T0329019

THE
IDYLLS
OF
THEOCRITUS

R. C. TREVELYAN

A TRANSLATION
of the
IDYLLS
of
THEOCRITUS

CAMBRIDGE
AT THE UNIVERSITY PRESS
1947

CAMBRIDGE
UNIVERSITY PRESS

University Printing House, Cambridge CB2 8BS, United Kingdom

Cambridge University Press is part of the University of Cambridge.

It furthers the University's mission by disseminating knowledge in the pursuit of education, learning and research at the highest international levels of excellence.

www.cambridge.org
Information on this title: www.cambridge.org/9781107432192

© Cambridge University Press 1947

First published 1947
First paperback edition 2014

A catalogue record for this publication is available from the British Library

ISBN 978-1-107-43219-2 Paperback

To

ELIZABETH MUNTZ

CONTENTS

INTRODUCTION

W E know scarcely anything about the life of Theocritus except what we are able to infer from his own poems. He would seem to have been a Syracusan, and to have been born somewhere about 310 B.C. It is probable that he spent several years between 290 and 283 B.C. in the island of Kos, as the pupil of the elegiac poet and critic, Philetas, and that he there became one of a literary circle which included Leonidas of Tarentum, Asklepiades and Nikias, the Milesian physician and poet. We have no evidence as to where he spent the next period of his life, between 283 and 275 B.C.; but his sixteenth Idyll, in which he courts the patronage of Hiero, the despot of Syracuse, was probably written in Sicily about the year 275. Part at least of the years between 274 and 270 B.C. would seem to have been spent at Alexandria, and Idylls xv and xvi would belong to this period. We know nothing of the closing years of his life, nor of where and when he died. The twenty-eighth Idyll is evidence that he once visited Miletus, and the fourth and fifth show that he was familiar with the neighbourhood of Croton in Southern Italy.

Apart from these few meagre conjectures and inferences, nothing more can be said about his life. Of the man himself, something, though not very much, is revealed in his seventh and sixteenth Idylls, and in the three lyrics at the end of the collection. For the artist, the poems themselves must speak. Although it is impossible to assign dates to any of the Idylls, except the sixteenth, it nevertheless seems likely that most of the pastoral poems were written during his Koan period, or at least before his residence at Alexandria. The eleventh Idyll is sometimes supposed to be his earliest; but the eighth and ninth, if, as I believe, they are his genuine work, may be still earlier. The more realistic and dramatic Idylls, such as ii, xiv and xv, probably belong to his maturity, and the same may be said of his epic experiments.

It is difficult to say how close a relation the pastoral poems of Theocritus bore to the songs of the Sicilian, South Italian and Koan country-folk of his day, because scarcely anything remains of Greek popular poetry and folk-song. Yet the realistic pastoral Idylls, such as iv, v and x, seem to show a direct acquaintance with the life of shepherds and herdsmen such as we very seldom find in the poems of later pastoral writers, whether classical or modern. Even the more artificial poems, such as the first and third, may well be literary refinements of peasant singing-matches and serenades, heard by Theocritus in his youth. Almost as important must have been the influence of Sophron, a Syracusan writer of the fifth century, whose prose mimes, now lost except for a few fragments, are known to have suggested to Theocritus both the form and the material for several of his pastoral Idylls, as well as for the *Sorceress* and the *Syracusan Women*, which are poems describing town life.

I have translated all the admittedly genuine Idylls, and such of the doubtful poems as seem to me to possess literary value. I have omitted Idylls xxiii and xxvi, because they are dull, stupid and worthless poems, and certainly not by Theocritus.

I have found it impossible to make my translation from any one of the published texts, and so have been obliged to form my own text, choosing, in corrupt passages, what appear to me to be the most plausible among the various readings proposed by scholars.

The metre which I have used, as the best equivalent for the hexameter, is an unrimed verse of seven accents. Its structure is the same as that of the normal half-stanza of the Scottish ballad, such as:

> And mony was the feather bed
> That flattered on the faem;
> And mony was the gude lord's son
> That never mair came haem.

It was also used in the form of rimed couplets by Chapman in his translation of the *Iliad*, and by other Elizabethan poets and translators. Blake, in his *Book of Thel*, was the first to dispense with rime, and vary the position of the cæsura.

I have found that a close translation of a Greek hexameter proves, on the average, to be of about the same length as this English verse, and so have been able to translate line for line with very little omission or expansion. The hexameter of Theocritus is undoubtedly a more beautiful, subtle and expressive medium; but the English metre has at least the merit of swiftness of movement, and can be given considerable variety by frequently changing the place of the chief cæsura, which naturally follows the fourth metrical accent. Sometimes I have omitted the syllable that should carry the fourth accent, as in the line:

> Sweet is the whispering music of yonder pine that sings.

This is an easy and natural variation of the metre, because there is a tendency in a line of seven accents for the first, third, fifth and seventh stresses to be slightly more prominent than the second, fourth and sixth, so that if the weak fourth stress be dropped, and compensated for by a slight pause, the fundamental rhythm is not impaired. This alternation of stronger and weaker stresses also causes a kind of undulation in the rhythm, which gives lightness and swiftness of movement to the verse.

It is no doubt always best to translate poems into poetry; but that is an ideal which is sometimes difficult of attainment; and so, in the case of two of the epic Idylls, and a number of the epigrams, I have preferred a faithful prose rendering to an unsatisfactory attempt in verse.

In the matter of transliterating the Greek proper names, I have found it impossible to be consistent. I myself prefer the Greek to the Latinised forms. Simaitha and Lakinion seem to me at least as beautiful as Simaetha and Lacinium, and just as harmonious in English verse. Where however our ears are so familiar with the Latin forms, that they have practically become English by adoption, as in the case of Syracuse, Cyclops, Cyprian, Lycidas, etc., I have thought it would be pedantical to insist on the Greek pronunciation. Whatever course I might take would be certain to displease somebody, so I have decided to make no attempt to please anyone except myself.

R. C. TREVELYAN

1925.

THE
IDYLLS
OF
THEOCRITUS

IDYLL I

THYRSIS

The Sicilian shepherd, Thyrsis, at the invitation of a goatherd, sings the 'Sorrows of Daphnis'. No complete version of this pastoral hero's legend has come down to us; but it would seem that Daphnis, after wedding the nymph Nais in his early youth, had boasted that he would never again be subdued by Love. So when the offended Aphrodite had inspired his heart with a passion for another nymph, Xenia, Daphnis refused to confess his love, and pined away to death, with his last words reproaching Aphrodite for her cruelty.

This beautiful Idyll has been the ancestor of a more numerous and distinguished progeny than any other poem of antiquity. Moschus, Virgil, Ronsard and Milton, followed by the innumerable flock of minor pastoral poets, have all imitated and borrowed from it with varying success; and its spirit, though not its form, may still be discerned in *Adonais* and *Thyrsis*.

THYRSIS. Sweet is the whispering music of yonder pine that sings
Over the water-brooks, and sweet the melody of your pipe,
Dear goatherd. After Pan, the second prize you'll bear away.
If he should take the hornèd goat, the she-goat shall you win:
But if he choose the she-goat for his meed, to you shall fall
The kid; and dainty is kid's flesh, till you begin to milk.
GOATHERD. Sweeter, O shepherd, is your song than the melodious fall
Of yonder stream that from on high gushes down the rock.
If it chance that the Muses take the young ewe for their gift,
Then your reward will be the stall-fed lamb; but should they choose
To take the lamb, then yours shall be the sheep for second prize.
THYRSIS. Now by the Nymphs, goatherd, I pray, will you not sit down there,
On yonder shelving hillock, among the tamarisks,
And pipe to me? I will stay here and tend your goats the while.
GOATHERD. That may not be; no, shepherd: we may not play the pipe
At noonday. It is Pan we dread; for at this very hour
He takes his rest wearied with hunting: and he's choleric;
Around his nostrils bitter wrath sits lurking evermore.
But, Thyrsis, you were wont to sing the tale of Daphnis' woe,
And in the pastoral Muse's art none has such skill as you.
Come then, let's sit beneath yon elm, over against the statues,
Priapus and the fountain Nymphs, there by the shepherd's seat
And the oak-tree grove; and if you will but sing as once you sang
In rivalry with that Chromis who came from Libya,

I'll give you for three milkings a goat, mother of twins,
Who yields two pailfuls every time, for all she feeds two kids.
A deep bowl of carved wood I'll give you too, rubbed with sweet bees-wax,
Two-eared and newly wrought, still smacking of the graver's tool.
Around the upper edges the winding ivy runs,
Ivy besprent with helicryse, and therewith intertwined,
Rejoicing in its golden berries, the proud tendril curls.
Within, a woman is designed, such as the Gods might fashion,
Clad in a robe, with snooded hair; and upon either side
Two men with fair long locks contending in alternate speech
One with the other; but her heart is touched by naught they say:
For now at one she glances with a smile, and now again
Flings to the other a light thought; while they, with heavy eyes
Long wearied out for love of her, are wasting toil in vain.
Beyond these there is carved an ancient fisherman, who stands
On a jagged rock, and busily the old man gathers in
His great net for a cast, like one who toils with might and main.
You'ld say that he was fishing with the whole strength of his limbs;
Such swelling sinews everywhere stand out around his neck;
For grey-haired though he be, his strength is worthy of youth still.
Then, but a little space beyond that sea-hardened old man,
Is a vineyard, richly laden with clusters fiery-red,
And guarding it a little lad upon a rough wall sits,
Two she-foxes on either side; one ranging up and down
The vine-rows, pilfering the ripe grapes; the other against the wallet
Is marshalling all her cunning, and vows she will not leave
That boy, till she has set him down to breakfast on dry crumbs.
But he with stalks of asphodel is plaiting a pretty cage
For locusts, binding it with a reed; nor cares he for his wallet,
Nor for the vines so much as in his plaiting he finds joy.
And all around the cup is spreading soft acanthus leaf,
A sight of varied loveliness, that will amaze your soul.
I bought it of a merchant who came from Calydon,
And the price I paid him was a goat and a great white cream-cheese.
Never yet has it touched my lip, but still unstained by wine
It lies. This bowl with all my heart would I bestow on you,
If you'll be kind and sing that song I yearn so much to hear.
I am in earnest. Come, friend; surely you will not hoard your song
Until you come to Hades where all things are forgot?

THYRSIS *sings*

Lead now, I pray, dear Muses, lead you the pastoral song.
Thyrsis am I of Etna; and sweet is the voice of Thyrsis.
Where were ye then, while Daphnis pined away, where were ye, Nymphs?
Haunting Peneios' lovely valleys, or the glens of Pindos?
For not by the great river of Anāpos were you dwelling,
Nor upon Etna's heights, nor yet by Akis' holy stream.
 Lead now, I pray, dear Muses, lead you the pastoral song.
For him the jackals howled, for him the wolves: the lion even
Came forth from the thicket to lament him when he died.
 Lead now, I pray, dear Muses, lead you the pastoral song.
Many a cow and many a bull stood round him where he lay,
Many a heifer and young calf, lowing for misery.
 Lead now, I pray, dear Muses, lead you the pastoral song.
First from the hills came Hermes, and said, 'Daphnis, my friend,
Who is it that is torturing thee? Whom so much dost thou love?'
 Lead now, I pray, dear Muses, lead you the pastoral song.
Came the herdsmen and the shepherds, and the goatherds came:
All of them asked what ailed him. Came Priapus too,
And said, 'Poor Daphnis, wherefore thus lie pining, while the maid
By every stream, through every grove is roaming up and down—
 Lead now, I pray, dear Muses, lead you the pastoral song.
—Seeking thee? Ah thou feckless boy, in love thou art but a fool.
A herdsman wast thou called, but now thou art like a sorry goatherd.
When a goatherd looks upon his flock sporting in wanton play,
His eyes grow wistful for regret that he was not born a goat;—
 Lead now, I pray, dear Muses, lead you the pastoral song.
—So thou, when thou beholdest how gaily the girls laugh,
Thine eyes grow wistful, since thou dost not join them in their dance.'
Yet to them all the herdsman answered naught, but still endured
His bitter love, aye, he endured it even to the fated end.
 Lead yet awhile, ye Muses, lead you the pastoral song.
But now the Cyprian Goddess[1] came, smiling in kindly mood,
Secretly smiling, though beneath pretence of heavy wrath.
'So, Daphnis, thou didst vow,' she said, 'thou would'st throw Love a fall:
Yet here is it not thou thyself by grievous Love art thrown?'
 Lead yet awhile, ye Muses, lead you the pastoral song.

---

[1] The Cyprian Goddess is Aphrodite.

Then at length answering her taunts spoke Daphnis: 'Cruel Cypris,
Vindictive Cypris, Cypris by mortal men abhorred,
Doubtless already thou dost deem my latest sun has set.
Nay, Daphnis even in Hades shall work Love bitter woe.
 Lead yet awhile, ye Muses, lead you the pastoral song.
Do they not tell how the herdsman loved Cypris? Get thee to Ida;
Get thee to thy Anchises.[1] There are oaks and galingale,
And there melodiously the bees flit humming round the hives.
 Lead yet awhile, ye Muses, lead you the pastoral song.
Adonis too is in his bloom. Either he tends the sheep,
Or shoots the hare, and chases the wild beasts every one.
 Lead yet awhile, ye Muses, lead you the pastoral song.
And then I'ld have thee go encounter Diomed,[2] and say:
"The herdsman Daphnis have I conquered; now fight *thou* with me."
 Lead yet awhile, ye Muses, lead you the pastoral song.
O wolves, O jackals, O ye bears that sleep in mountain caves,
Farewell! The herdsman Daphnis you shall never meet with more,
Never in forest, glade or grove. Fare thee well, Arethusa,
And all you streams that down the vale of Thymbris flow so fair.
 Lead yet awhile, ye Muses, lead you the pastoral song.
I am that Daphnis, he who drove the kine to pasture here,
Daphnis who led the bulls and calves to water at these springs.
 Lead yet awhile, ye Muses, lead you the pastoral song.
O Pan, Pan, whether thou art on the high hills of Lykaios,
Or whether o'er great Mainalos thou roamest, hither come
To the Sicilian isle, and leave the tomb of Helike,
And Lykaonides' lofty cairn, which even the Gods revere.
 Break off, I pray, ye Muses, break off the pastoral song.
Come, lord, and take this shapely pipe, fragrant with honeyed breath
From the sweet wax that joins it, curved to fit the lip so well.
As for me—down to Hades Love is haling me already.
 Break off, I pray, ye Muses, break off the pastoral song.
Bear violets henceforth, ye brambles, and ye thistles too,
And upon boughs of juniper let fair narcissus bloom;
Let all things be confounded; let the pine-tree put forth figs,
Since Daphnis lies dying! Let the stag tear the hounds,

---

[1] Anchises and Adonis were both loved by Aphrodite.
[2] Diomedes, according to Homer (*Iliad* v, 330), fought with Aphrodite, and wounded her in the hand.

And screech-owls from the hills contend in song with nightingales.'
  Break off, I pray, ye Muses, break off the pastoral song.
These words he spoke, then said no more: and him would Aphrodite
Fain have raised back to life; but no more thread for the Fates to spin
Was left him: down to the stream[1] went Daphnis: eddying waves closed o'er
The man loved by the Muses, whom every Nymph held dear.
  Break off, I pray, ye Muses, break off the pastoral song.

And now give me the she-goat and the bowl, that I may milk her
And pour forth to the Muses. O Muses, fare you well,
And again farewell. Another day a sweeter song I'll sing you.
GOATHERD. Thyrsis, may your fair mouth for this be filled and filled again
With honey and the honey-comb; and may you eat dried figs
From Aigilos; for more lovely than the cricket's is your song.
See, here's the bowl; and mark, my friend, how savoury it smells.
In the well-spring of the Hours you might think it had been dipped.
Come here, Kissaitha!—She is yours to milk.—Beware, you kids;
Skip not so wantonly, or you'll have the he-goat after you.

---

[1] The stream of Death.

IDYLL II

THE SORCERESS

Simaitha, forsaken by her lover, the young athlete Delphis, endeavours by various magic rites to draw him back to her house, invoking the Moon by her three names of Selene, Hekate and Artemis. Afterwards she tells the Goddess the tale of her love, and of her desertion by her lover, and finally vows to poison him, if her charms should fail.

It is uncertain whether the scene of this Idyll is the island of Kos, or of Rhodes, or some town on the Karian coast. The subject, and to some extent the form, are said by the Greek commentator, or Scholiast, to have been suggested to Theocritus by one of the lost prose mimes of Sophron, who however had given Simaitha's attendant, Thestylis, a share in the dialogue. Virgil's imitation in his eighth Eclogue is a frigid academic exercise, with none of the passion, the realism and the poetic beauty, which make this Idyll perhaps the greatest love-poem in the whole of classical and modern literature.

WHERE are those laurels? Bring them, Thestylis—and the love-charms too.
Wreath the cauldron with a crimson fillet of fine wool;
That I may cast a fire-spell on the unkind man I love,
Who now for twelve whole days, the wretch, has never come this way,
Nor even knows whether I be alive or dead, nor once
Has he knocked at my doors, ah cruel! Can it be that Love
And Aphrodite have borne off his roving heart elsewhither?
To Timagētos' wrestling school tomorrow will I go,
And find him and reproach him with the wrong he is doing me.
But now by fire-magic will I bind him. Thou, O Moon,
Shine fair; for to thee softly, dread Goddess, will I chant,
And to infernal Hekate, at whom the very whelps
Shudder, as she goes between the dead men's tombs and the dark blood.
Hail, awful Hekate! and be thou my helper to the end,
Making these charms prove no less potent than the spells of Circe,
Or of Medea, or the gold-haired sorceress Perimede.

O magic wheel, draw hither to my house the man I love.
First in the fire barley grains must burn. Come, throw them on,
Thestylis. Miserable girl, whither now are flown thy wits?
Even to thee am I, vile wretch, become a thing to scorn?
Cast them on, and say thus, 'the bones of Delphis I am casting.'

O magic wheel, draw hither to my house the man I love.
Delphis has wrought me anguish, so against Delphis do I burn

This laurel shoot: and as it catches fire and crackles loud,
And is burnt up so suddenly, we see not even the ash,
So may the flesh of Delphis be wasted in the flames.
　　O magic wheel, draw hither to my house the man I love.
Even as now I melt this wax by the aid of Hekate,
So speedily may Myndian Delphis melt away through love.
And even as turns this brazen wheel by Aphrodite's power,
So restlessly may he too turn and turn around my doors.
　　O magic wheel, draw hither to my house the man I love.
Now will I burn the bran. Yea thou, Artemis, thou hast power
To move Hell's adamantine gates, and all else that is stubborn.
Thestylis, hark, the dogs are baying now throughout the town:
At the cross-roads is the Goddess. Quick, beat the brazen gong.
　　O magic wheel, draw hither to my house the man I love.
Behold, the sea is silent, and silent are the winds;
But never silent is the anguish here within my breast,
Since I am all on fire for him who has made me, unhappy me,
Not a wife, but a worthless woman, a maiden now no more.
　　O magic wheel, draw hither to my house the man I love.
Thrice do I pour libation, Goddess, and thrice speak this prayer:
Whether it be a woman lies beside him, or a man,
Let such oblivion seize him, as on Dia[1] once, they tell,
Seized Theseus, when he quite forgot the fair-tressed Ariadne.
　　O magic wheel, draw hither to my house the man I love.
Horse-madness is a herb that grows in Arcady, and maddens
All the colts that range the hills, and the fleet-footed mares.
Even so frenzied may I now see Delphis: to this house
May he speed like a madman from the oily wrestling school.
　　O magic wheel, draw hither to my house the man I love.
This fringe from his mantle did Delphis lose, which now
I pluck to shreds and cast it into the ravenous fire.
Woe's me, remorseless Love, why clinging like a fen-born leech
Hast thou sucked from my body the dark blood every drop?
　　O magic wheel, draw hither to my house the man I love.
A lizard will I bray, and bring him a deadly draught tomorrow.
But now, Thestylis, take these magic herbs, and secretly
Smear them upon his upper lintel, while it is night still,
Then spit, and say, 'It is the bones of Delphis that I smear.'

　　　　　[1] Dia is another name for the island of Naxos, one of the Cyclades.

O magic wheel, draw hither to my house the man I love.

Now that I am alone, whence am I to bewail my love?
Wherefrom begin my tale? Who was it brought this woe upon me?
  Anaxo, daughter of Euboulos, bearing the mystic basket,
Passed this way in procession to the grove of Artemis,
Many a wild beast thronging round her, among them a lioness.
  Bethink thee of my love and whence it came, O holy Moon.
So Theucharidas' Thracian nurse, who since has gone to bliss,
But then was living at our doors, besought and entreated me
To come and see the pageant; and I, poor luckless fool,
Went with her in a linen gown, a lovely trailing robe,
Over which I had thrown a cloak that Klearista lent me.
  Bethink thee of my love and whence it came, O holy Moon.
And now, half way along the road, as we passed Lykon's house,
I saw Delphis and Eudamippos walking side by side.
Their beards were more golden than flower of helichryse,
And far more brightly shone their breasts than thou thyself, O Moon;
For from the wrestling school they came, fresh from their noble toil.
  Bethink thee of my love and whence it came, O holy Moon.
O then I saw, and fell mad straight, and my whole heart was fired,
(Woe is me!) and my comely cheeks grew pale; nor did I heed
That pageant any longer. And how I came back home
I know not; but a parching fever seized me and consumed me,
So that I lay pining in bed for ten days and ten nights.
  Bethink thee of my love and whence it came, O holy Moon.
And often pale as boxwood grew the colour of my flesh,
And the hairs kept falling from my head, till what was left of me
Was naught but skin and bones. To whom did I not now resort?
What old crone's house did I not visit, who was skilled in spells?
But that way remedy was none; and time fled swiftly by.
  Bethink thee of my love and whence it came, O holy Moon.
So at last I told the whole truth to my serving-maid, and said:
'Go, Thestylis; find me some cure for my sore malady.
Wholly am I become (woe's me!) the Myndian's slave. But go,
Go now and lie in wait for him at the school of Timagētos;
For there it is he most resorts, there that he loves to lounge.
  Bethink thee of my love and whence it came, O holy Moon.
And when you are sure no one is near, nod to him silently,

And say, "Simaitha calls you," and bring him hither straight.'
So did I speak; and she went hence, and brought back to my house
Delphis, the sleek-limbed youth. But I, no sooner was I ware
Of his light footfall, as he crossed the threshold of my door,—
   Bethink thee of my love and whence it came, O holy Moon.
—In every limb I froze more cold than snow, and from my brow
The sweat came streaming forth and trickling down like drops of dew.
Nor had I strength to speak one word, not so much as a child's
Whimpering murmur, when it calls to its mother dear in sleep;
But all my lovely body turned as stiff as any doll.
   Bethink thee of my love and whence it came, O holy Moon.
Then, seeing me, that heartless man, with eyes fixed on the ground,
Seated himself upon my bed, and sitting there spoke thus:
'Truly, Simaitha, your command by just so much outstripped
My coming, when you called me hither to your house, as I
Outstripped charming Philinos not long since in the race.
   Bethink thee of my love and whence it came, O holy Moon.
For of myself I should have come, yes, by sweet Love, I should,
With comrades two or three besides, as soon as it was night,
Carrying in my tunic-folds apples of Dionysus,
A wreath of poplar garlanding my brows, the holy tree
Of Herakles, with twining purple ribbons all enlaced.
   Bethink thee of my love and whence it came, O holy Moon.
And had you welcomed me, why then, it had been joy; for famed
Am I among my comrades for beauty and speed of foot.
Had I but kissed your lovely mouth, I would have slept content.
But if you had repulsed me, and bolted fast the door,
With axes and with torches you would then have been besieged.
   Bethink thee of my love and whence it came, O holy Moon.
And now to the Cyprian in truth first do I owe my thanks;
But after Cypris, it is you, Lady, who from the flames
Have rescued me, when thus you sent to invite me to your house,
Half-consumed as I am. Yea Love enkindles oft a blaze
More fiery than Hephaistos' self, the God of Lipara:—
   Bethink thee of my love and whence it came, O holy Moon.
—And he drives with evil frenzy both the maiden from her bower,
And the bride from her lord's embrace, leaving the bed yet warm.'
So did he speak: and I, that was so easy to be won,
Took him by the hand and drew him down to the soft couch.

And soon limbs at the touch of limbs grew love-ripe, and our faces
Glowed warmer still and yet more warm, and we whispered sweet words.
So, not to lengthen out my tale and weary thee, dear Moon,
The greatest deeds of love were done, and we both reached our desire.

  Since then so long as yesterday no fault had he to find
In me, nor I in him. But now today there came to me
The mother of our flute-player Philista, and of Melixo,
Just when the horses of the Sun were climbing up the sky,
Bearing forth from the Ocean the Dawn with rosy arms.
After much other gossip she said Delphis was in love;
But what desire has mastered him, for a woman or a man,
She was not sure, but knew this only, that he was ever pledging
His love in cups of unmixed wine, and at last rushed away
Swearing he'ld crown with garlands the threshold of his dear.
Such is the tale the woman told me; and it is the truth.
For he was wont to visit me three or four times each day,
And often would he leave his Dorian oil-flask with me here.
But now 'tis twelve whole days since I so much as looked on him.
Can he have found some other solace, and forgotten me?

  Now with these philtres will I strive to enchant him. But if still
He should grieve me, at Hell's gate soon, by the Fates, he shall knock:
Such evil drugs to work his bane here in a chest I store,
Whose use, dear Mistress, an Assyrian stranger taught me once.
But thou, Goddess, farewell, and turn thy steeds to the Ocean stream,
And I will endure my misery still, even as I have borne it.
Farewell, bright-faced Selene; and farewell too, ye stars,
That follow the slow-moving chariot of the tranquil Night.

IDYLL III

THE SERENADE

A goatherd, learned in mythological love-tales, serenades his Amaryllis, in vain.
Virgil must have known this lovely poem by heart, and imitates it not unhappily in
several of his Eclogues.

I WILL go serenading Amaryllis, while my goats,
With Tityrus to herd them, go browsing o'er the hill.
My well-belovèd Tityrus, pasture my goats awhile,
And to the spring-head lead them, my Tityrus: but beware
Yon tawny Libyan he-goat's tricks, else he'll be butting you.

O beautiful Amaryllis, why no longer from your cave
Do you peep forth to greet me, your beloved? Do you hate me then?
Can it be I appear snub-nosed, dear nymph, when seen from close?
A jutting-bearded Satyr? You will make me hang myself.
See here ten apples I have brought you, fetched down from the tree
From which you bade me fetch them. I will bring ten more to-morrow.
Look on my heart-tormenting grief. Would that I might become
Yon booming bee, and enter so your cavern, steering through
The ivy and the feathery fern, wherein you lie embowered.
Now I know Love. A cruel god is he: a she-lion's breasts
He sucked, and in a forest his mother nurtured him,
Since with slow fire he burns me thus, smiting me to the bone.
O beautifully glancing—but all stone! O dark-browed Nymph!
Around me, your own goatherd, fling your arms, that I may kiss you.
Even in empty kisses there is a sweet delight.
Soon you will make me tear this garland into little shreds,
This ivy wreath, dear Amaryllis, that I keep for you,
Twining it with rose-buds and sweet-smelling parsley-leaves.
Oh misery! What will be my fate, poor wretch! Will you not answer?
I'll strip my cloak off and leap down to the waves from yonder cliff,
Whence Olpis, the fisherman, watches for tunny shoals:
And if I perish—well, at least that will be sweet to you.
I found it out not long ago, when wondering if you loved me
I smeared the love-in-absence, and the petal would not stain,
But creased and withering there it lay on the soft of my arm.

A peasant too, Paraibatis, the sieve-divining witch,
Gathering herbs the other day, told me the truth, that I
Have wholly set my heart on you, while you care naught for me.
Listen: I keep for you a white she-goat, mother of twins,
Which Mermnon's daughter begs of me, dark-skinned Erithakis:
And she shall have it, since you choose to trifle with my love.
I feel a twitch in my right eye. Can it be that portends
That I shall see her? I will lean against yon pine and sing.
It may be she will look on me. She is not adamant.

He sings

Hippomenes, when he would win the maiden for his bride,
Entered the race with apples in his hands. But Atalanta
No sooner saw, but fell mad straight, and leapt into deep love.
Melampos too, the soothsayer, from Othrys drove the herd
To Pylos, and for Bias won a lovely bride to lie
Within his arms and bear his child, the wise Alphesiboia.
Did not Adonis, shepherding his flock upon the hills,
Lead on the beauteous Cytherea down frenzy's path so far
That even now, dead though he be, she clasps him to her breast?
Enviable I deem the sleeper of that changeless slumber,
Endymion:[1] and I envy too Iasion, Goddess dear,
Who won such bliss as the profane in love may never know.

My head is aching; but 'tis naught to you. I'll sing no more:
I will fall down and let the wolves devour me where I lie.
May this prove no less sweet to you than honey down your throat.

[1] Endymion was beloved by the Moon-goddess, Artemis; Iasion by Demeter.

IDYLL IV

THE HERDSMEN

In this rustic mime the goatherd Battos chaffs the simple-minded Korydon upon the wretched condition of his absent master Aigon's cattle. The scene is in Southern Italy, near Croton. In its realism and humour this Idyll resembles the fifth, and both are probably inspired by lost mimes of Sophron.

BATTOS. Korydon, tell me, who is it owns those cows? Is it Philondas?

KORYDON. No, they are Aigon's: he it is who gave them me to pasture.

BATTOS. Do you find a way to milk them all at nightfall on the sly?

KORYDON. Nay, the old man keeps his eye on me and puts the calves to suck.

BATTOS. But he himself, the cowherd, to what land has he vanished?

KORYDON. Haven't you heard? He's been shipped off by Milon to the Alphēos.[1]

BATTOS. And when did Aigon ever set his eyes on wrestler's oil?

KORYDON. They say he rivals Herakles in lustiness and strength.

BATTOS. And mother says that I'm a better man than Polydeukes.[2]

KORYDON. When he went hence, he took a spade and twenty of his sheep.

BATTOS. As well might Milon coax the wolves to raven against the flock.

KORYDON. Hark how his heifers, longing for their master, low for grief.

BATTOS. Aye, the poor wretches, what a sorry herdsman they have found!

KORYDON. Poor beasts indeed! No longer have they any will to graze.

BATTOS. Look at that young cow yonder! There's nothing left of her
But bones. Pray, does she feed on dewdrops, like a grasshopper?

KORYDON. No by Earth! but sometimes I graze her by Aisāros' banks,
And feed her with fine handfuls of green and tender grass;
Otherwhile she wantons in the shadowy dales around Latymnos.

BATTOS. How lean is yonder red bull too! Would that Lampriades' folk
May get, when next they sacrifice to Hera in their deme,
Just such a beast as that! They're all a dirty blackguard lot.

---

[1] The Panhellenic games took place at Olympia, a town of Elis, on the banks of the river Alpheos.

[2] Polydeukes was the famous boxing demigod. Part of the training of athletes was shovelling sand, and their main diet was meat.

KORYDON. And yet to Stomalimnon's lake I drive him, and the meads
Of Physkos, and beside Neaithos' river, where grow all
The herbs he loves, goatwort and fleabane and sweet-smelling balm.
BATTOS. Alackaday, poor Aigon! your very kine will go
To Hades, while you are thus in love with a luckless victory;
And mildewed is the pipe which once you fashioned for yourself.
KORYDON. Not his pipe, by the Nymphs, not so; for when he went to Pisa,[1]
He left it me to keep; and I am something of a minstrel.
Right well can I strike up the songs of Glauke and of Pyrrhos;
And I sing the praise of Croton, and 'A fair town is Zakynthos,'
And 'Fair too is Lakinion that fronts the dawn,' where Aigon,
The boxer, by himself alone devoured eighty cakes.
And there he caught the bull by the hoof, and dragged him from the mountain,
And gave him to Amaryllis, while the women shrieked aloud
For terror; but the herdsman burst into a mighty laugh.
BATTOS. O beautiful Amaryllis, thee alone, though thou be dead,
I'll ne'er forget. Dear are my goats: so dear in death art thou.
Ah me, too cruel was the daemon that disposed my fate.
KORYDON. Take heart, dear Battos. Better luck perchance will come to-
    morrow.
While there is life there's hope. Without hope are the dead alone.
Zeus one day shows a clear and cloudless sky, the next he rains.
BATTOS. Yes, I'll take heart.—Drive them uphill, those calves. The wretched
    beasts!
They're nibbling at the olive shoots.—Sitt! you with the white hide!
KORYDON. Sitt! Kymaitha! Can't you hear me? Off with you up the hill!
I'll soon be after you, by Pan; and a bad end will I give you,
If you won't clear out quickly. Look! there she comes creeping back.
Would I had here my crooked staff, to give you a cudgelling!
BATTOS. O Korydon, in the name of Zeus, pray look. See, here's a thorn
Has just now pierced my foot, beneath the ankle, here. How deep
These spindle-thorns can go! Plague take your heifer! She it was
That I was gaping after, when I got pricked. D'you see it?
KORYDON. Yes, yes! and now I've got him 'twixt my nails. Look, here he
    comes.
BATTOS. What a tiny wound it is, and what a big man it can master!

[1] Pisa, a town not far from Olympia, originally instituted and controlled the
Panhellenic festival.

KORYDON. When you walk in hilly places, never go barefoot, Battos;
For on these hillsides everywhere brambles and thorns grow thick.
BATTOS. Pray tell me, Korydon, is it true the silly old gaffer still
Sports with that black-browed darling, whom once he used to dote on?
KORYDON. Aye, just as much as ever, friend. But two days gone I chanced
To catch them at the very byre, when he had her in his arms.
BATTOS. Well done, lusty old lecher! 'Tis plain you are near akin
Both to the Satyrs and the slim-shanked Pans, whose feats you rival.

IDYLL V

KOMATAS AND LAKON

Lakon, a shepherd, seated beside a brook beneath a wild-olive, and Komatas, a goatherd, who is lying a little distance away under a pine-tree, after exchanging various ribaldries, challenge each other to a singing match. They call to Morson, a wood-cutter, to be their judge, and he, after listening to fourteen couplets from each competitor, awards the prize to Komatas. The scene is again in Southern Italy, near Thurii and the ancient site of Sybaris, which had been destroyed more than two hundred years before by the Crotonians. Virgil has modelled his third Eclogue upon this Idyll.

KOMATAS. Beware, my goats, keep clear of yonder shepherd of Sibyrtas,
That rascal Lakon, him that stole my goat-skin yesterday.
LAKON. Away there, won't you? from the spring! Sitt, my lambs! Don't you see
Komatas there, the man who stole my pipe the other day?
KOMATAS. Your pipe indeed! Whenever did *you*, Sibyrtas' slave,
Possess a pipe? Why, can it be that you're no more content
To sit with Korydon and whistle on your flute of straw?
LAKON. The pipe that Lykon gave me, sir freeman! And what goat-skin
Did Lakon ever filch away from *you*? Tell me, Komatas.
Why, even your master, Eumāras, never had one to sleep in.
KOMATAS. It's the skin Krokylos gave me, the dappled one, that day
He sacrificed the goat to the Nymphs; and you, you knave, were pining
With envy even then, and now at last have stripped me bare.
LAKON. Now by the sea-shore Pan, it was not Lakon, son of Kalaithis,
Who robbed you of that coat of skin: or else, sir, if I lie,
May I run mad and leap into the Krathis from yon rock.
KOMATAS. Now by the Nymphs, good man, I swear, by these Nymphs of the mere,
(So may they evermore be kind and gracious to me still!)
It was not I, Komatas, who stole that pipe of yours.
LAKON. If I believe you, may I suffer all the woes of Daphnis!
However, if you'll lay me a kid—it's not much of a stake,
I own—but still I'll sing against you, until you cry 'enough.'
KOMATAS. A pig once matched his skill against Athene. Look, I've staked
My kid. Come then, it's your turn now to stake a fine fat lamb.

LAKON. And how, you cunning fox, can such a bet be fair between us?
Who would choose hair to clip instead of wool? And who'ld prefer,
When he might have a young milch goat, to milk a filthy bitch?
KOMATAS. One who's so sure he can defeat his neighbour as *you* seem,
Is like a wasp buzzing against a cicala's song. Well, since
You deem the kid is no fair stake, there's the he-goat. Begin.
LAKON. Why in such haste? You're not on fire. More sweetly will you
    sing,
If you'll sit here within this grove, beneath the olive tree.
See, yonder is cool water trickling down; here is fresh grass
And this soft bed of leaves, and here locusts are chattering.
KOMATAS. I'm not in haste: nay, but I'm sorely vexed that you should dare
To look me in the face with such bold eyes, you whom I used
To teach when you were still a child. See what becomes of kindness!
Yes, rear up wolf-cubs, rear up dogs, to be devoured by them!
LAKON. And what good thing can I remember ever to have learnt
Or heard from you, you envious, unseemly manikin?
KOMATAS. When I did that to you that made you cry for pain; the while
My she-goats yonder bleated, and the he-goat leapt on them.
LAKON. May your grave be no deeper, you hunchback, than that thrust!
But come now, come this way, and you shall sing your last goat-song.
KOMATAS. No, yonder I will not go. See, here are oaks, here's galingale,
And here melodiously the bees flit humming round the hives:
Two wells of cool water are here; and birds upon the tree
Are warbling; and beyond compare the shade is pleasanter
Than where you lie; and from above the pine drops cones around me.
LAKON. Ah, but if you come hither, upon lambs' wool shall you tread,
And upon fleeces softer than slumber. But those goat-skins
Which you have over there, stink fouler even than yourself.
And as an offering to the Nymphs a great bowl of white milk
Will I set out, yes, and another of sweet olive oil.
KOMATAS. Nay, but if you come hither, you shall tread on delicate fern
And flowering mint; and skins of she-goats shall be strewn beneath you
Four times softer than the fleeces of those lambs of yours.
And I'll set out eight pails of milk as an offering to Pan,
And eight bowls too of combs filled full of honey in every cell.
LAKON. Stay there then, and begin the match: sing your song where you are.
Tread your own ground. You're welcome to your oaks. But who's to judge?
Aye who? Might but Lykōpas, the neatherd, come this way!

KOMATAS. No, I don't want *him* here, not I. But if you like, we'll call
That fellow over there, not far from you, the woodcutter,
Who's busy gathering heather into bundles. Morson it is.
LAKON. Let's shout then.

KOMATAS.   Give him a call yourself.

LAKON.   Ho, friend, come hither, pray,
And listen awhile; for there's a match on foot between us two,
Which is the better singer. So, good Morson, when you judge,
You should neither show me favour, nor yet be too kind to him.
KOMATAS. Yes, by the Nymphs, dear Morson, neither award Komatas
What is not justly his, nor yet unduly favour Lakon.
This flock of sheep, my friend, belongs to the Thurian Sibyrtas,
And these goats which you see are owned by Eumāras of Sybaris.
LAKON. Now in the name of Zeus, you knave, who asked you if 'twas I
Or Sibyrtas that owned the flock? What a babbler you are!
KOMATAS. Most excellent of men, I like to speak the truth in all things:
Boasting is not my way. But you are far too fond of railing.
LAKON. Come, say your say, and then have done, and let our friend go
    home
Alive. O Paian, how you do love chattering, Komatas!

They sing

KOMATAS. The Muses love me far more dearly than the minstrel Daphnis;
And well they may, for not long since I offered them two kids.
LAKON. Aye, but Apollo dearly loveth *me*; and a fine ram
For him I feed, against the Karnean feast that's drawing near.
KOMATAS. Save two, the she-goats that I milk have every one borne twins.
The maiden looks on me, and 'alas,' she says, 'do you milk alone?'
LAKON. Aha! but Lakon has wellnigh a score of baskets filled
With cheese, and lies amid the flowers clasping the lad he loves.
KOMATAS. Klearista pelts the goatherd with apples, as he drives
His she-goats by, and murmurs some sweet word with pouting lips.
LAKON. And smooth-cheeked Kratidas, when he meets me shepherding my
    flock,
Maddens me, with his glistening hair dancing about his neck.
KOMATAS. Nay, who would liken the dog-thorn or windflower to the rose,
That blossoms in its rose-bed beneath the garden wall?
LAKON. Nor should one liken medlars to acorns; for to these
The oak-tree gives a bitter husk, but those are sweet as honey.

KOMATAS. But I will give my maiden a ring-dove, which I'll steal
To-morrow from the juniper-tree; for there it sits and broods.

LAKON. But I, when next I shear the dusky ewe, will freely give
The soft fleece to my Kratidas, to make of it a cloak.

KOMATAS. Sitt! Leave those olives. Here, you bleaters, it's here you must
   feed,
Upon this shelving hillock, among the tamarisks.

LAKON. Won't you leave that oak alone, you Kōnaros, you Kinaitha?
Graze here, where Phalāros feeds, where the hill fronts the dawn.

KOMATAS. A pail of cypress-wood is mine, and a mixing bowl, a work
Worthy of Praxiteles; and I keep both for my girl.

LAKON. And I've a dog that loves the flock, one that can throttle wolves:
Him will I give my boy, to chase wild beasts of every kind.

KOMATAS. Ye locusts that come leaping across our fence, beware;
See that you ravage not my vines; for they are young and tender.

LAKON. Behold, ye crickets, how I chafe the goatherd with my taunts.
'Tis even so you are wont to vex the reapers with your songs.

KOMATAS. I hate those foxes with their bushy tails, that always come
Prowling round Mikon's fields at nightfall, pilfering his grapes.

LAKON. Even so I hate those beetles, that come flitting on the breeze
And settle down in swarms to devour the ripe figs of Philondas.

KOMATAS. Do you call to mind that merry trick I played you once, and how
You grinned and writhed so nimbly, and clung fast to yonder oak?

LAKON. That I remember not; but how Eumāras bound you there
And gave you a good dusting once, that can I well recall.

KOMATAS. Already, Morson, somebody's growing bitter, can't you see?
Go now in haste and pluck him squills from some old woman's grave.[1]

LAKON. I too am stinging somebody, Morson, you see that plain.
Be off to the Hales now and dig for roots of cyclamen.

KOMATAS. Let Himera flow with milk instead of water; and thou, Krathis,
With wine mayest thou run purple, and may thy reeds bear fruit.

LAKON. Let Sybaris' fountain flow, I pray, with honey, and at dawn
In honey, not in water, let the maiden dip her jar.

KOMATAS. My goats browse upon goatswort and leaves of cytisus;
They tread on lentisk, and lie down beneath the arbute-trees.

LAKON. But for *my* sheep to browse on, there is honeyed balm in plenty,
And shrubs of cistus flowering like roses everywhere.

---

[1] Squills were a remedy for bilious melancholy, and cyclamen bulbs possessed
medicinal virtues.

KOMATAS. No more do I love Alkippe, for last night she would not take
My face between her hands and kiss me, for that dove I gave her.
LAKON. But with Eumēdes I am deep in love; for when I brought
That pipe to give him, he thanked me with such a lovely kiss.
KOMATAS. It is not right, Lakon, for jays to strive with the nightingale,
Nor yet hoopoes with swans. Poor fool, how you love quarrelling!
MORSON. Enough! I bid the shepherd cease. And it's to you, Komatas,
Morson awards the lamb. And when you offer her to the Nymphs,
Be sure you send to Morson a good portion of her flesh.
KOMATAS. Yes, by Pan, so I will. Now snort for triumph, you whole herd
Of young he-goats; and I too, see how long and loud I'll laugh
In mockery of that shepherd, that Lakon, now at last
I've won the ewe-lamb. You shall see me leap sky-high for joy.
Cheerly, my butting she-goats! Tomorrow will I take you
Down to the lake of Sybaris and there dip you everyone.
You there, you white-faced he-goat, I'll cudgel you if you dare
Mount any of my she-goats, before I've sacrificed
The lamb to the Nymphs.—At it again! If I don't cudgel you,
Let henceforth not Komatas but Melanthios be my name.[1]

[1] Melanthios was the unfaithful goatherd whom Odysseus mutilated and killed for
his treachery (Homer, *Odyssey* XXII, 474).

IDYLL VI

DAPHNIS AND DAMOETAS

The herdsmen, Daphnis and Damoetas, meet and contend together in song. First Daphnis makes believe that he is chaffing Polyphemus the Cyclops for his love of Galateia the sea-nymph; then Damoetas replies in the person of the Cyclops, who, as in Idyll xi, has little resemblance to the savage cannibal of the *Odyssey*, but appears in the character of a simple-minded Sicilian shepherd. Daphnis, here and in Idyll viii, is the legendary Sicilian herdsman of the first Idyll. The poem is addressed to Aratos, the literary friend of Theocritus, who appears in Idyll vii. His name has been omitted from the second line of the translation.

DAMOETAS and the herdsman Daphnis had driven each his flock
To feed together in one place. Golden down fledged the chin
Of one; half grown was the other's beard. Beside a water-spring
Both of them in the summer noon sat down and thus they sang.
Daphnis began the singing, for the challenge came from him.

'See you not, Polyphemus, how Galateia is pelting
Your flock with apples? Fool-in-love she calls you, a goatherd clown.
Yet no glance will you give her, hard of heart, but still you sit
Piping so sweetly. There again, look how she pelts your dog,
The faithful guardian of your sheep. Into the sea he peers
And barks, while in the pretty waves, that plash so tranquilly,
His image is reflected as he runs along the sand.
Take good care, or else he'll leap right at the maiden's legs,
As she comes from the sea, and rend her fair flesh with his teeth.
See how she stands coquetting there, light as the dry winged seeds
Blown from a thistle in the lovely summer's noonday heat.
If a man love, she flies him; if he love not, she pursues,
And moves her last piece from the line:[1] for truly in Love's eyes
Often, O Polyphemus, what is not fair seems fair.'

Then after him Damoetas struck a prelude and sang thus:
'I saw it, yes, by Pan, when she was pelting at my flock:
She escaped not me, nor this one beauty of mine, wherewith to the end

---

[1] A metaphor taken from an ancient game, somewhat resembling draughts.

I'll look at her. Let Tēlemos, that evil-boding seer,[1]
Carry his evil bodements home to keep them for his children.
Nay, 'tis to punish and torment her that I will not look,
Giving it out I love some other girl: this she has heard,
And pines with jealousy for me, by Paian, and from the deep
Comes in a frenzy forth to gaze upon my caves and herds.
I hissed to my dog to bark at her; for when I was in love,
He used to whine for joy and rub his muzzle on her knees.
Perchance, seeing me treat her thus time after time, she'll send
Some messenger: but I'll shut my doors, until she swear to make me
With her own hands upon this isle a lovely nuptial bed.
For truly not ill-favoured is my face, as they pretend.
Not long ago I looked into the sea, when it was calm,
And beautiful my beard seemed, beautiful my one eye,
If I have any judgment; and the gleaming of my teeth
Whiter than Parian marble was reflected in the sea.
Then, to avoid the evil eye, I spat thrice in my breast,
A charm once taught me by that ancient crone, Cotyttaris.'

Damoetas, when he thus had sung, kissed Daphnis, and therewith
Gave him a pipe, while Daphnis gave his friend a shapely flute.
Damoetas fluted, and the herdsman Daphnis played the pipe,
And soon the calves were dancing about the tender grass.
Neither had won the victory: they were both invincible.

[1] The seer Telemos had prophesied that Polyphemus would be blinded by Odysseus (*Odyssey* IX, 508). 'This one beauty of mine' is the eye in the middle of the Cyclops' forehead.

IDYLL VII

THE HARVEST-HOME

Simichidas, who is no other than Theocritus himself, describes how he was once walking with two friends from the town of Kos to a harvest festival at a farm six or seven miles away, near the river Haleis, and how, before they were half way on their road, they fell in with Lycidas, a goatherd. After a friendly challenge from Simichidas, each sings a pastoral poem of his own, and then Lycidas parts company with his three friends, who at length arrive at the farm, and take part in the harvest festival.

The following note was pencilled by Macaulay on the margin of this Idyll in his Theocritus. 'This is a very good idyll. Indeed it is more pleasing to me than almost any other pastoral poem in any language. It was my favourite at College. There is a rich profusion of rustic imagery about it which I find nowhere else. It opens a scene of rural plenty and comfort which quite fills the imagination—flowers, fruits, leaves, fountains, soft goat-skins, old wine, singing birds, joyous friendly companions,—the whole has an air of reality which is more interesting than the conventional world which Virgil has placed in Arcadia.'

There is good reason to believe that most of the persons mentioned in this Idyll were actual friends of Theocritus. We know that he spent several years at Kos as the pupil of the pastoral poet Philetas. Other members of this school were Asklepiades, Leonidas of Tarentum and Alexander of Aitolia, and scholars are of opinion that Sikelides, Lycidas and Tityrus were their respective pseudonyms. Whoever Aratos may have been, he was certainly not the author of the once famous but now unreadable astronomical poem. But we have no need of historical conjecture and research in order to enjoy the varied charm and loveliness of this Idyll.

It chanced that Eukritos and I set out to walk one day
Towards the Haleis from the town: Amyntas made a third.
For the two sons of Lykōpeus were holding the harvest feast
Of Deo,[1] Phrasidemos and Antigenes, good fellows
Of fine old lineage, dating back to Klytia and that Chalkon,
Who caused Bourĩna's fountain to well forth at his feet,
Pressing stoutly against the rock his knee: and there hard by
The poplars and the elm-trees, weaving a shady grove,
Sprang up, an overarching roof of branches and green leaves.
Not half way had we journeyed yet, nor had the tomb of Brasilas
Risen to view, when by the Muses' grace we overtook
A Kydonian,[2] a man of worth, travelling the same road,
Called Lycidas, a goatherd, as none could fail to know
At first glance, for like nothing but a goatherd did he seem.

[1] Deo was a name of Demeter.   [2] Kydonia was a town in Crete.

A tawny skin, stripped from a thick-haired he-goat's shaggy back,
He wore upon his shoulders, of fresh rennet reeking still.
Across his breast an ancient well-worn tunic was strapped round
By a broad belt, and a crooked staff from a wild olive tree
He held in his right hand: and gently with a smiling eye
He spoke to me, while laughter still played about his lips:
　'Whither by noon, Simichidas, are you toiling along thus,
When even the very lizard in the stone wall is asleep,
And the tomb-crested larks no more are flitting to and fro?
Are you bidden to a banquet, that you stride along so fast?
Or else to tread some neighbour's vintage? For your speed is such,
That all the stones in the road are ringing stricken by your boot.'
　'Dear Lycidas,' I answered him, ''tis you that all men say
Among herdsmen and harvesters have far the greatest skill
In playing on the pan-pipes: and it delights my heart
To hear this said. Yet to my thinking I should have some claim
To be your rival. Now our journey leads to a harvest-home,
Where friends are making festival to the fair-robed Demeter
From the first-fruits of their increase; for with wealth of barley grain
The Goddess in rich measure has filled their threshing-floor.
But come, since we are sharers alike of road and morn,
Let us sing pastoral lays: perchance each will delight the other.
For I too serve the Muses; their clear-voiced mouth am I.
All call me best of minstrels; but I am not credulous;
No, by the Earth, for to my mind I cannot conquer yet
In song that rare Sikelides of Samos, nor Philetas,
But vainly like a frog against cicalas I contend.'
　Thus did I speak to gain my end: and with a kindly laugh
The goatherd said: 'I offer you this crook, because I know
You are a sapling Zeus has moulded wholly in truth's mould.
Even as I loathe your builder who strives to raise a house
As lofty as the topmost peak of Mount Oromedon,
So all birds of the Muses do I loathe, that croak and cackle
Against the Chian minstrel,[1] wasting their toil in vain.
But come let us begin forthwith our pastoral melodies,
Simichidas: and I first—well, friend, see if this chance to please you,
This ditty which I worked out not long since on the hills.

[1] The Chian minstrel is Homer.

He sings

   Fair voyage to Mytilene shall befall Ageänax,
When the Kids are in the Western sky, and the South wind is chasing
The wet waves, and Orion stands with his feet on the sea,
If he will but save Lycidas, who in Aphrodite's fire
Is scorched; for burning is the love that consumes me for him.
The halcyons will calm the ocean waves and lull the winds
Of South and East, that stir the sea-weed far up on the shore,
The halcyons that are dearest to the green-haired Nereïds
Of all the birds that from the salt sea waters take their prey.
Thus may the season smile upon Ageänax as he sails
To Mytilene, and may his ship come safely home to port.
And I upon that day will set a garland on my head
Of anise, or of roses, or of white violets,
And the best wine of Ptelea will I pour forth from the bowl,
As I lie before the fire, where beans are roasting in the embers.
And high as to the elbow thick-strewn shall be my couch
With sweet fleabane and asphodel and curling parsley leaves.
Thus will I drink luxuriously with Ageänax in my thoughts
Draining each wine-cup with firm lip even to the very dregs.
   Two shepherds, from Acharnae one, the other from Lykōpe,
Shall be my flute-players; and beside me Tityrus shall sing
How once Daphnis the herdsman loved Xenia the nymph,
And how the mountain grieved for him, and the oak-trees sang his dirge
(The oaks that grow along the banks of the river Himeras),
When he lay wasting like a streak of snow beneath tall Haimos,
Or Rhodope, or Athos, or far-off Caucasus.
   And he shall sing how once the goatherd was enclosed alive
In a great coffer by his lord's outrage and cruel spite;
And how the blunt-faced bees, as from the meadows they flew home
To the fragrant chest of cedar-wood, fed him with tender flowers,
Because with sweet nectar the Muse had steeped his lips.
   O fortunate Komatas, such joys indeed were thine;
Yea, prisoned in the coffer, by the bees thou wast fed
With honey-comb, and didst endure thy bondage a whole year.
Would that thou hadst been numbered with the living in my days,
That so I might have grazed thy pretty she-goats on the hills,
Listening to thy voice, whilst thou under the oaks or pines
Hadst lain, divine Komatas, singing sweet melodies.'

So far he sang, then made an end; and after him in turn
Thus did I speak: 'Dear Lycidas, many things else the Nymphs
Have taught me too, while I was pasturing kine among the hills,
Good songs, that fame perchance has brought even to the throne of Zeus.[1]
But one there is, the best of all, which now to do you honour
I'll sing. Do you then listen, since the Muses love you well.

He sings

On Simichidas the Loves have sneezed: for truly the poor wretch
Loves Myrto just as dearly as the goats love the Spring.
But Arātos, whom Simichidas holds best of all his friends,
Hides in his heart the longing for a boy. Aristis knows
(That best and worthiest man, whom Phoebus' self would joy to see
Standing beside his tripods and singing lyre in hand),
He knows how love for a boy is burning Arātos to the bone.
O Pan, lord of the pleasant pastures of Mount Homole,
I pray thee, bring him unbidden to my friend's longing arms,
Whether it be the delicate Philinos, or some other.
And if thou wilt do this, O darling Pan, may nevermore
The Arcadian children whip thee with squills about thy ribs
And shoulders, when too little meat is left them on thy altar.
But if otherwise thou shouldst decree, then may bites set thy nails
Scratching thy skin all over, and on nettles mayst thou couch.
On the Edonian mountains in midwinter mayst thou dwell
Lodging beside the river Hebros near to the Great Bear.
But mid the farthest Aethiops in summer mayst thou range,
Beneath the Blemyan mountain cliff, whence Nile is seen no more.

But ye, leaving the pleasant fount of Hyetis and Byblis,
And Oikeus' hill, the lofty shrine of golden-tressed Dione,[2]
O ye winged Loves, rosy as blushing apples, hither come,
Pierce, I pray, with your arrows Philinos the desired,
Pierce him, that miserable wretch, who pities not my friend.
And yet he's but a pear that's over-ripe, and the girls cry,
"Ah welaway Philinos! fading is thy fair bloom!"
Come then, Arātos, let's no more stand watching at his gates,
Nor wear our feet away; but let the cock that crows at dawn
Give others over to be chilled by numbing misery.

[1] Some scholars think that by 'the throne of Zeus' Theocritus meant the throne of
Ptolemy II, King of Egypt.
[2] Dione here means Aphrodite, though it is really the name of Aphrodite's mother.

Alone let Molon wrestle, friend, with anguish such as that.
But our concern be peace of mind: some old crone let us seek,
To spit on us for luck and keep unlovely things afar.
  Thus I sang; and the goatherd, with the same kindly laugh,
Gave me the crook, in token of our brotherhood in the Muses.
Then slanting off towards the left he took the road to Pyxa,
While with the pretty boy Amyntas, Eukritos and I
Turned to the farm of Phrasidemos; and arriving there
We soon were lying joyously couched upon soft deep beds
Heaped with scented rushes and vine-leaves newly stripped.
And high above our heads there swayed and quivered many a branch
Of poplar and of elm-tree, while close beside us welled
The sacred water gushing from the cavern of the Nymphs.
Amid the shadowing foliage the brown cicalas chirped
And chattered busily without pause; and far away was heard
From the dense bramble thicket the tree-frog's fluted note.
Larks and thistle-finches sang, the turtle dove was moaning:
About the running water hovered the tawny bees.
All things breathed the scent of teeming summer and ripe fruits.
Pears at our feet lay fallen, and apples at our sides
Were rolling in abundance; and the plum-tree's tender boughs
Drooped overburdened with their load of damsons to the earth;
And mouth of jars, for four years sealed with resin, were unstopped.
  Ye Nymphs of Castaly, that haunt the steep Parnassian hill,
Did ever aged Cheiron in Pholos' rocky cave
Set before Herakles a bowl with such a vintage filled?
Did ever such a draught of nectar beguile that shepherd lout
Who dwelt beside Anāpos, and pelted ships with crags,
Strong Polypheme, and set his feet capering about his folds?—
Such a draught as ye Nymphs that day made stream for us beside
Harvest Demeter's altar, upon whose mound of corn
May it be mine once more to plant the great fan, while she sits
And smiles upon us, holding sheaves and poppies in each hand.

IDYLL VIII

DAPHNIS AND MENALKAS

Daphnis the herdsman, and Menalkas the shepherd, meet together on the hills and contend in pastoral song. The first part of the contest consists of four alternate pairs of elegiac quatrains. They afterwards each sing four hexameter couplets. Daphnis wins the prize. Some scholars suspect that this Idyll was written by an imitator of Theocritus; but one would like to think that so beautiful a poem was his genuine, though probably youthful, work. Even if it be a patchwork, Theocritus may well have done his own patching.

BEAUTIFUL Daphnis, so 'tis told, herding his kine one day
Met with Menalkas, shepherding his flock on the high downs.
The hair of both was golden; young striplings were they both;
Both of them skilled at pipe-playing, at singing both were skilled.
Then looking upon Daphnis, Menalkas spoke the first:
'Daphnis, thou herd of lowing kine, wilt sing a match with me?
I swear I'll vanquish thee in song as easily as I choose.'
Then answering his challenge these words did Daphnis say:
'Thou pipe-player Menalkas, shepherd of fleecy sheep,
Ne'er shalt thou vanquish me, not though you sing till your heart break.'
MENALKAS. Then wilt thou put it to the proof? A wager wilt thou lay?
DAPHNIS. Yes, I will put it to the proof; a wager I will lay.
MENALKAS. And what shall be our stake, what prize that may be worth
    our while?
DAPHNIS. I'll stake a calf, and thou a lamb, grown to its mother's height.
MENALKAS. No, never will I stake a lamb; for a hard one is my father,
My mother too. At nightfall they number the whole flock.
DAPHNIS. But what then wilt thou stake, and what's to be the victor's gain?
MENALKAS. My lovely reed-pipe with nine notes, that I myself have made,
Joined with white beeswax equally both above and below.
That would I lay; but naught that is my father's will I stake.
DAPHNIS. I also have just such another reed-pipe with nine notes,
Joined with white beeswax equally both above and below.
It was but yesterday I made it; and this finger here
Still hurts me, for I pierced it with the point of a split reed.
MENALKAS. But who's to judge between us? Whom shall we ask to listen?
DAPHNIS. How about yonder goatherd? Suppose we call him hither—
That fellow with the white-faced dog that's barking among the kids.

So the boys shouted, and the goatherd came to listen for them:
The boys sang, and the goatherd consented to be judge.
It was clear-voiced Menalkas drew the lot to sing first,
Then Daphnis followed, taking up in turn the answering strain
Of pastoral song; and thus it was that Menalkas began.

They sing

MENALKAS. Ye dells and rivers, offspring of the God, if ever heretofore
  The flute-player Menalkas sang a melody you loved,
Then feed his lambs with bounteous will; and if perchance Daphnis one day
  Come hither with his calves, no less a welcome may he find.

DAPHNIS. Ye springs and meadows of fresh grass that grows so sweetly, if
    indeed
  Daphnis in his song can rival the very nightingales,
Then fatten ye this herd of his; and should Menalkas hither drive
  His sheep-flock, may he too rejoice in pasture without stint.

MENALKAS. There doth the ewe, there do the goats bear twins, and there
    the bees fill full
  Their hives with honey, and the oaks grow loftier than elsewhere,
Wherever lovely Milon's feet have trodden; but if he depart,
  Then withered grows the shepherd, and withered grows the grass.

DAPHNIS. Everywhere spring, and everywhere pasturage, and on every side
  Udders swollen with milk, and younglings fostered by their dams,
Wherever lovely Nais may go wandering; but if she depart,
  Parched is he that feeds the kine, and parched his cattle too.

MENALKAS. O he-goat, thou the lord of the white flock, go now where the
    deep wood
  Is deepest...(Hither, you blunt-faced kids! come hither to the well!)
O stump-horn, thither go, for there is he, and 'Milon,' shalt thou say,
  'A herdsman once was Proteus, though a God, and herded seals.'

DAPHNIS. ... (*A quatrain is missing here*)[1]

MENALKAS. Not for me the land of Pelops, nor ever be it mine to hoard
  Golden talents, nor to run more fleetly than the wind;
But neath this rock I'll sit and sing, holding thee in my arms, and watch
  Our mingled flocks, gazing far out o'er the Sicilian sea.

DAPHNIS. For trees a dreaded evil is the stormy tempest, drought for
    streams,

---

[1] The arrangement of these quatrains is doubtful; but it seems most probable that
the third quatrain of Daphnis has been lost.

The snare for birds, and for the wildwood beasts the hunter's net,
But for a man the longing for a gentle maiden. O Father Zeus,
  It is not I alone have loved; thou hast loved woman too.

So sang the boys, each in his turn rivalling the other's song.
And now Menalkas began thus to chant the final lay:
MENALKAS. Spare my kids, wolf, I pray thee: spare the mothers of my flock.
Do me no wrong, so young am I to tend so great a herd.
Ah my good dog, Lampouros, how soundly you are slumbering!
When you go shepherding with a lad, you should not sleep so sound.
Fear not, my ewes, to crop your fill of yonder tender grass.
Before you are tired of feeding, it will have grown again.
Sitt! Browse on, browse on, and fill your udders all with milk;
Some for your lambs, and some for me, to press in my cheese-crates.

After him Daphnis lifted his tuneful voice and sang:
DAPHNIS. Yesterday from her cave a girl with meeting eyebrows spied me,
As I drove past my calves, and cried, 'How pretty he is, how pretty!'
Yet never a word to tease her did I deign to answer back,
But fixed my eyes upon the ground and plodded on my way.
Sweet is the lowing of the heifer, and sweet smells her breath,
And sweet to lie by a running stream beneath a summer sky.
As acorns are a pride to the oak, to the apple-tree its apples,
So to the heifer is her calf, to the cowherd his kine.

Such were the songs those children sang, and thus the goatherd spoke:
'Sweet is thy mouth, O Daphnis, and delectable thy voice.
To hear thee sing is better than tasting honeycomb.
Take thou the pipes, for thou art conqueror in the singing match.
And if thou wilt but teach me, while I'm pasturing my herd,
As a wage for your teaching you shall have this stump-horn goat,
That every time you milk her fills the pail right to the brim.'
Oh then the lad clapped hands for joy to have won the victory,
And leapt and capered, as a fawn capers around its dam.
But the other's heart smouldered away and was distraught with grief,
Sorrowing like a maiden that is wed against her will.
Thenceforth among the shepherds Daphnis became the first,
And wedded the Nymph Nais, while yet in his youth's prime.

IDYLL IX

DAPHNIS AND MENALKAS

At the request of the poet, Daphnis and Menalkas each sing a short poem describing the delights of the herdsman's and of the shepherd's life. The poet rewards them with presents, and sings a few lines of his own in praise of poetry.

The genuineness of this Idyll has been doubted, but on insufficient grounds. Probably the first six lines are a spurious addition: the rest may well be the early work of Theocritus. Cholmeley, with some plausibility, regarded the last nine lines as 'a tail piece not to Idyll IX alone, but to a small bucolic collection made by Theocritus himself after leaving Kos'.

COME, Daphnis, sing; and do thou first begin the pastoral song;
Begin thou first, and let Menalkas follow, when you have set
The calves beneath their dams and driven the bulls among the kine.
Then let them browse together, wandering through the leafy copse,
But never straying from the herd. And do thou sing to me
From this side, while from the other let Menalkas make reply.
DAPHNIS. Sweet is the lowing of the calf, and sweetly the cow lows,
Sweetly the cowherd with his pipe, and I too sweetly sing.
By the cool brook is strewn my leafy couch, whereon are heaped
The pretty skins of my white calves, that once the South-west wind
Dashed from the cliff when they were browsing on the arbute tree.
Thus for the scorching summer's heat as little do I care
As a lover cares to heed the words of father or of mother.

Thus to me Daphnis sang, and thus Menalkas answered him.
MENALKAS. Etna, my mother, in a lovely cave do I make my home
Within the hollow rocks; and there everything that in dreams
We may behold, is mine, both many sheep and many goats,
Whose skins are strewn a fleecy couch beneath my head and feet.
In the oak-wood fire paunches are boiling, and dry chestnuts roasting
On winter nights; nor for the wintry season do I care
One whit more than a toothless man for nuts, when cake is by.

Then did I clap my hands and straightway gave them each a gift,
A staff to Daphnis, one that in my father's field had grown,
Self-shapen, such that even a craftsman might have found no fault;
But to the other a lovely spiral shell, that once I caught
On the Ikarian rocks, and cut the fish into five shares
For five of us to feast on. And the youth winded his conch.

Now fare ye well, ye pastoral Muses; and make known the songs
That once, when I consorted with those herdsmen swains, I sang.
No more upon my tongue-tip let a tell-tale pimple grow.[1]

Cicala to cicala is dear, and ant to ant,
And kestrels dear to kestrels, but to me the Muse and song.
Of song let my whole house be full; for not more sweet is sleep,
Nor sudden spring, nor sweeter are flowers to the bees:
Even so dear to me the Muses. All whom they regard
With gracious eyes, Circe may never harm them with her spells.

[1] The Scholiast tells us that 'when such a pimple appears upon your tongue women are wont to say that you have not paid back what was entrusted to you'. The meaning of the line would then seem to be that Theocritus has received his inspiration from the Muses, so until he has published his poems, and proved that he has put the gift of the Muses to a good use, his debt to them will remain unpaid.

IDYLL X

THE REAPERS

In this rustic mime the satirical Milon teases his simple-hearted fellow-reaper, Battos, about his passion for a Syrian farm-wench. Battos then sings a sentimental love-song, and Milon a string of popular rural maxims.

MILON. Tell me, you toilsome clodhopper, what ails you now, poor wretch?
Can you neither cut your swathe straight, as you were wont of old,
Nor keep time with your neighbours as you reap, but must fall out
Like a ewe that straggles from the flock, when a thorn has pricked her foot?
What will be left of you by dusk, nay earlier, when noon's past,
If now at the start your sickle makes no bigger bites than that?
BATTOS. Milon, you who can reap so late, true chip of stubborn stone,
Has it never been your lot to long for one that was away?
MILON. Never. What right has a labouring man to long for what's not there?
BATTOS. Then has it never been your lot to lie awake for love?
MILON. Nay, God forbid! It's ill to let a dog once taste of pudding.
BATTOS. Yet I, Milon, have been in love the best part of ten days—
MILON. 'Tis plain you draw from the wine-jar. With me even sour stuff's scarce.
BATTOS. —And so the fields before my door since seed-time lie unhoed.
MILON. But which of the girls is plaguing you?
BATTOS.   It's Polybotas' maid,
Who was piping to the reapers on Hippokoön's farm last week.
MILON. Well, God's found out the sinner. You've got what you've long wished for.
You'll have a skinny locust now to clasp you all night long.
BATTOS. I see you mean to gird at me. There's other Gods are blind
Besides Plutos:[1] there's reckless Love for one. So don't talk big.
MILON. Talk big! Not I. But come now, you can still reap your swathe,
And strike up a love-ditty to the girl. You'll find your toil
The sweeter so. I know you were a singer in old days.
BATTOS. (*He sings*). Ye Muses of Pieria, sing the slender maid with me:
For whatsoe'er ye Deities touch, you turn to loveliness.
   Charming Bombyka, Syrian they do call thee everywhere,
Lean, sunburnt: it is I alone that call thee honey-fair.

----

[1] Plutos was the God of Wealth.

Dark is the violet, and dark the scriptured iris grows;
Yet when we're making garlands, the first we choose are those.
The goat pursues the cytisus, the wolf pursues the goat,
The crane follows the plough; but I on thee do madly doat.
Ah would that all the fabled wealth of Croesus now were mine,
Then graven in gold we two should stand in Aphrodite's shrine,
Thou with thy flutes, and with a rose or apple in thy hand,
I in fine robes, shod in Amyklian buskins new and grand.
Charming Bombyka, knuckle-bones thy feet are, shapely and white.
Syrup thy voice; but ah, thy ways, they are past my power to indite.
MILON. Truly we had no notion what fine songs the clod could make.
How cunningly he measured out and shaped his melody!
Alas for this man's beard, which to no purpose I have grown!
Yet hear these too, these couplets of Lityerses the divine.

He sings

Demeter, rich in fruit and grain, grant thou that this year's crop
Be quickly reaped and gathered in, and fruitful beyond hope.
Bind tight the sheaves, ye bandsters, lest passers-by should say,
'These are mere men of fig-wood. 'Tis wages thrown away.'
See that the cut end of your sheaf be laid to face the West
Or the North wind: for thus it is the grain will fatten best.
They that thresh corn should shun the noonday sleep. When the sun's high,
Then is the time that chaff from straw will part most easily.
But reapers should start toiling when the lark leaves his nest,
And cease work when he sleeps; but in the noonday heat should rest.
The frog's life is most jolly, my lads; he has no care
Who shall fill up his cup; for he has drink enough to spare.
You miserly steward, boil us better lentil soup. Take heed,
You're sure to cut your finger, splitting that cummin seed.[1]

It's songs like that, that men should sing who labour in the sun.
But for that starveling love of yours, you clodhopper, 'twere fit
To drone it in your mother's ear, when she wakes in bed at dawn.

---

[1] The Greeks called a stingy man a cummin-splitter, or, as Bacon paraphrases it,
'a carver or divider of comine seed, which is one of the least of seedes',

IDYLL XI

THE CYCLOPS

Theocritus reminds his enamoured friend Nikias, the physician of Miletus, that song is the only remedy for the pains of love, illustrating this truth by the example of Polyphemus, when he was tormented by love for the sea-nymph Galateia.

The Scholiast tells us that Nikias wrote an answering poem that began with these lines:

> Yes, there, Theocritus, you spoke the truth; for the Loves have taught
> Many men to be poets, who were museless souls before.

This Idyll has had many imitators, among whom Virgil in his second Eclogue is the most successful. Elsewhere (Ecl. viii, 38–43) he echoes lines 25–27 of this poem, in a passage of which Macaulay writes in a letter: 'I think that the finest lines in the Latin language are those five which begin,

> Sepibus in nostris parvam te roscida mala—

I cannot tell you how they struck me. I was amused to find that Voltaire pronounces that passage to be the finest in Virgil.'

THERE is no other medicine, Nikias, against Love,
Neither by way of ointment nor of plaster, take my word,
Save the Pierian Muses. A gentle remedy
And sweet is that for men to use, yet very hard to find.
Well indeed must you know this, physician as you are,
And dearly loved beyond all others by the Muses nine.
'Twas thus at least our countryman the Cyclops eased his pain,
That Polyphemus of old time, when he loved Galateia,
And upon cheek and lips as yet his beard was scarce grown.
Not with apples nor roses did he woo, nor locks of hair,
But with sheer frenzies; all things else he reckoned as mere trifling.
Often from the green pastures would his sheep unshepherded
Wander back to the fold, while he, singing his Galateia,
There on the weed-strewn sea-beach all day from early dawn
Would sit and pine, nursing within his breast a cruel wound,
Dealt him by mighty Cypris, whose shaft had pierced his heart.
Nevertheless that cure he found; and seated on the crest
Of a tall rock, and gazing towards the sea, thus would he sing:
'O white Galateia, wherefore thus cast off the man who loves you?
Whiter to look upon than curds, more delicate than a lamb,
Than a young calf more skittish, plumper than ripening grape!
Wherefore do you keep coming thus, whene'er sweet slumber takes me,

Only to vanish straight, whene'er sweet slumber lets me go,
Fleeing me swifter than a ewe, when the gray wolf she spies?

   I fell in love with you, dear maid, that very day when first
You came here with my mother,[1] to gather iris flowers
Upon the mountain, and 'twas I went with you as your guide.
Thenceforth, once having seen you, I could not cease to love,
Nor can I yet. But naught you care, no by Zeus, naught at all.

   I know, beautiful maiden, why it is you shun me thus.
It is because from one ear to the other, right across
The whole width of my forehead, one long shaggy eyebrow runs,
With but one eye beneath; and broad is the nose above my lip.
Nevertheless, though I be such, a thousand sheep I feed,
And from these do I draw and drink milk of the very best.
And cheese neither in summer nor in autumn do I lack,
Nor in winter's depth, but always overladen are my crates.
Then I am skilled in piping as no other Cyclops here,
And of thee, my dear sweet apple, and of myself I sing
Many a time at dead of night. Moreover eleven fawns
I am rearing for you, all with brows crescent-marked, and four bear-cubs.

   Nay, come to me, and nothing, that is yours now, shall you lack.
Leave the blue breakers of the sea to gasp against the land.
More sweetly will you pass the night beside me in my cave.
There do laurels grow, and there the slender cypress trees,
There the dark ivy, there the vine with its sweet clustering grapes;
There are cool streams of water, that from her white snows drawn
Forest-girt Etna sends me hither, an ambrosial drink.
To such delights who would prefer the sea-waves for a home?

   But if my body seem too rough and shaggy for your taste,
Well, neath the ashes on my hearth oak-logs are ever smouldering,
And gladly would I suffer you to singe my very soul,
And this one eye of mine, the dearest treasure I possess.
Ah me, would that my mother at my birth had given me gills,
That so I might have dived down to your side and kissed your hand,
If your lips you would not let me: and I had brought you then
Either white snowdrops, or the soft, scarlet-petalled poppy.
Nay, but these blow in summer, those in the winter months.
So I could never bring you both these kinds at the same time.

---

[1] The parents of Polyphemus were Poseidon and the sea-nymph Thoōsa.

But now, my darling maiden, now I'll learn at least to swim
(If hither sailing on a ship some stranger chance to come),
And so discover why you love to dwell thus in the deep.
  Oh come forth, Galateia, and coming straight forget,
Even as I now sitting here, to go back to your home.
Be content to go shepherding and milk the flocks with me,
And learn to set the cheeses, pouring tart rennet in.
It is my mother alone who wrongs me; yes, 'tis her I blame.
Never once has she spoken to you one kind word for me,
And that although day after day she saw me wasting thinner.
I'll tell her that my head and both my feet with pain are throbbing.
Thus will I make her suffer, since I am suffering too.
  O Cyclops, Cyclops, whither are your wits gone wandering?
Nay go and weave your baskets, and gather tender shoots
To feed your lambs. If you did that, far wiser would you be.
Milk the ewe that's beneath your hand. Why pursue one who shuns you?
You'll find perchance another and a fairer Galateia.
Many are the girls that call to me to play with them by night,
And each of them laughs softly, if I deign to give ear.
It's plain enough, I too on land seem to be somebody.'
  Well, thus it was that Polyphemus shepherded his love
With song, and found ease better so than if he had spent gold.[1]

---

[1] Than if he had fee'd a doctor to cure him: a palpable hit at Dr Nikias.

IDYLL XII

THE BELOVED YOUTH

This charming lyrical poem is inspired, like Idylls xxix and xxx, by passionate friendship for a youth. Though the emotion is doubtless sincere, its expression would seem to be conventional, and is probably reminiscent of lost lyrics by Ionic love-poets, such as Anacreon.

So thou hast come at length, dear lad, with the third night and morn;
Thou hast come: but a longing lover grows old in a single day.
As spring is sweeter than the winter, the apple than the sloe,
As the ewe wears a shaggier fleece than doth the lamb she bore,
As a maiden is more to be desired than a thrice-wedded wife,
As a fawn is nimbler than a calf, and as of all winged fowl
It is the clear-voiced nightingale that sings the sweetest song—
By so much does thy coming make me glad, as a wayfarer
Who hastens under a shady oak tree out of the scorching sun.
Would that with even breath the Loves might breathe upon us two,
That so we might become a song for all men yet unborn.
'These two once lived in friendship amid folk of former days,
One the *Inspirer*, as those say who use the Amyklian tongue,[1]
The other called the *Listener* in the speech of Thessaly.
They loved each other with an equal yoke. Verily then
There were true men of gold, when the belov'd paid back his debt.'
O Father Zeus, and you, ye deathless ageless Gods, grant this:
Two hundred generations hence let someone bring me down
These tidings beside Acheron's irremeable stream:
'Even now the love, that was between thee and thy gracious friend,
Is alive on the lips of all, but of the young men most.'
Nay, of such things the heavenly Gods have power to dispose
According to their will: but when I praise thee for thy beauty,
No boil to punish perjury shall burgeon on my nose.
For if ever thou tormentest me, forthwith thou heal'st the wound,
Doubling my bliss, and sending me with over-measure home.

   Nisaean men of Megara, ye champions of the oar,
Blest be your habitations, since ye honoured above all
Diokles,[2] your Athenian guest, who loved his friend so well.

[1] Amyklae was a town near Sparta; so the 'Amyklian tongue' means 'Doric'.
[2] Diokles fell in battle, while saving a youth whom he loved.

Ever in early spring the youths, gathering around his tomb,
Vie with each other who shall win the prize for the best kiss.
And whosoever presses lip most sweetly upon lip,
Crowned with victorious garlands to his mother he goes home.
Blessed is he who judges the kisses of those lads.
Sure he must offer many a prayer to bright-faced Ganymede,
That his lips may be sensitive as the Lydian stone, whereby
The money-changers test their gold, if it be base or true.

IDYLL XIII

HYLAS

This poem, like the eleventh Idyll, is addressed to Nikias. The story of Hylas was a favourite theme with both the Greek and Latin poets. 'Cui non dictus Hylas puer?' as Virgil complains; although he himself had been an offender in his sixth Eclogue. This Idyll of Theocritus is the best, as well as the earliest in date, of the Hylas poems that have come down to us.

NOT for us only, Nikias, as we supposed, was Love
Begotten, whosoever of the Gods was once his sire:
Nor yet are we the first to whom beauty seemed beautiful,
We that are men that perish, and look not on the morrow.
Nay, but Amphitryon's hero son,[1] whose heart was strong as brass,
Who abode the fierce lion's onset, he too once loved a lad,
The comely Hylas, him whose locks fell down in braided curls,
And taught him all things as a father teaches his dear son,
All whereby he himself had come to hardihood and renown.
Never was he apart from him, neither at day's high noon,
Nor when the white steeds of the dawn were racing up the sky,
Nor yet when twittering chickens look bedward longingly,
While on the smoke-browned henroost their mother flaps her wings;
And all this that the lad might grow moulded to his desire,
And nobly yoked with him might come to be a true man too.

But when to fetch the Golden Fleece Jason was setting sail,
And with him were embarking the noblest of the land,
Whom out of every city he had chosen as worthiest,
There came with them to rich Iolkos that great man of toil
Whose mother was Alkmena, the Midian heroine,
And with him Hylas came on board Argo, the well-benched ship,
That on the dark-blue Clashing Rocks grazed not, but like an eagle
Darted through and sped onward o'er the wide sea to the mouth
Of Phasis; and thenceforth the Rocks stand fixed as reefs for ever.

At the rising of the Pleiades, what time the upland fields
Are pasturing the young lambs, and spring already is on the wane,
Then did that godlike company of heroes turn their thoughts
To seafaring, and sat down to their oars in Argo's hull.
Three days the South wind blew, and now to Hellespont they came,

[1] Herakles was the son of Amphitryon and Alkmena.

And harboured within Propontis, where the Kiānian steers
Drive the furrow broad and deep, and wear the ploughshare bright.
So there they went on shore, and two from every bench made ready
Their evening meal; then for them all one common couch they strewed:
For there a meadow lay that gave them bedding and to spare,
And thence they cut the pointed rush and deep marsh-galingale.
Meanwhile the fair-haired Hylas, bearing a brazen vessel,
Was gone in search of water for Herakles to drink
And steadfast Telamon; those two were comrades, and together
Supped ever at one table. Erelong he espied a spring
In a low-lying field, and all around it many rushes
Were growing, and glossy swallow-wort, and fresh green maidenhair,
And luscious parsley, and deer-grass creeping o'er the marshy soil.
And in the water's midst the Nymphs were joining hands to dance,
The sleepless Nymphs, those goddesses feared by the country folk,
Eunika, and Malis, and Nykheia with her springtide glance.
Now as the boy was reaching forward eagerly to dip
His wide-mouthed pitcher in the well, they all clung to his hand,
For love had fluttered all their tender hearts when they beheld
The Argive lad. So down he tumbled into the dark water
Headlong, as when a fiery star falls headlong from the sky
Into the deep, and haply to his mates a seaman calls,
'Come, shorten sail, my lads: the wind is freshening for a storm.'
    Then the Nymphs took the child and set him weeping on their knees,
And strove to soothe his grief with kind and comfortable words.
Meantime Amphitryon's son was troubled at the boy's delay,
And went forth carrying his bow in Scythian fashion bent,
And the great club that always he grasped in his right hand.
Thrice he called 'Hylas!' loudly as his deep throat could bellow,
And thrice did the boy answer; but from beneath the water
Thin came his voice; and though so near, yet far away he seemed.
As when a bearded lion hears the bleating of a fawn
Far off upon the hills, a ravening lion, and from his lair
Bounds forth to snatch the ready meal that waits him, even so
Did Herakles rush wildly through trackless thorny brakes,
Ranging over much country in his longing for the boy.
Reckless are lovers. Ah what toils, wandering through hills
And thickets, he endured, while Jason's quest was all forgot!
The ship lay ready with her tackle raised and stores embarked;

Yet at midnight the heroes were lowering the sails
To wait for Herakles. But he, wherever his feet might lead him,
Was roaming with a frenzied heart, rent by a cruel God.

   So thus is loveliest Hylas numbered among the Blest.
But for a runaway the heroes taunted Herakles,
Because he forsook Argo and her thirty pairs of oars.
So on foot he reached the Kolchians and the inhospitable Phasis.

IDYLL XIV

THE LOVE OF KYNISKA

The scene of this mime is probably Kos. Aischines tells his friend, Thyŏnichos, how his mistress Kyniska has thrown him over for a handsome neighbour, and talks of going off to serve as a soldier abroad. Thyŏnichos recommends Ptolemy as the best paymaster for a free man. This and the next Idyll show Theocritus at his greatest as a modern realistic poet.

AISCHINES. Good day to you, friend Thyŏnichos!

THYŎNICHOS. The same to Aischines!

AISCHINES. What an age since we met!

THYŎNICHOS. Why yes, an age. But what's your trouble?

AISCHINES. I'm out of luck, Thyŏnichos.

THYŎNICHOS. So that's why you're so lean,
And your moustache wants trimming, and your hair's all lank and dry;
Just like that Pythagorean who came here t'other day,
Pale-faced and bare-footed, an Athenian, so he said.
He too was in love, I'm thinking—with a good wheaten loaf.

AISCHINES. You must always have your jest, good friend. Well it's fair
    Kyniska flouts me.
I shall go mad soon, mark my words. I'm but a hair's-breadth from it.

THYŎNICHOS. That's you all over, Aischines my dear: a shade too hasty,
And must have all things your own way. But tell me, what's your news?

AISCHINES. The Argive and myself, and that Thessalian horse-tamer
Agis, and the soldier Kleunïkos, had all met
To drink together at my house. I had killed a brace of pullets,
And a sucking pig, and broached them a fragrant jar of Bibline,
Just four years old, yet near as fresh as when it left the press.
Truffles were served, and shellfish: it was a jovial drinking-bout.
Well, when we'd been some time at work, we agreed that each in turn
Should pledge his fancy in unmixed wine; but each must name his toast.
So we all drank and called our toasts, as was agreed: yet she
Names nobody, though I was there. How think you I liked *that*?
'Won't you speak? Met a wolf?' joked someone.[1] 'A clever guess!' she
    cried,
And blushed. You could have easily lit a torch at her face.

[1] There was a superstition that anyone who met a wolf became dumb. Kyniska's new friend was called Lykos, which means 'wolf'.

It is Wolf, Wolf it is, the son of neighbour Labas yonder,
Tall, and soft, and handsome, at least many think him so.
He it was she was pining for with that notorious love.
Aye, and a breath of this came once in a whisper to my ears;
But I never made enquiry, bearded fool that I am!
    Well, by this time the four of us were drenched deep in our cups,
When that Larissan fellow struck up 'My friend the Wolf,'
A Thessalian song, and sang it through, the blackguard. But Kyniska
Suddenly broke out weeping, and shed a whole wet flood,
Just like a girl of six years old who longs for her mother's lap.
Then I—you know me, Thyōnichos—struck her a blow on the cheek,
And again another, with clenched fist: and she caught up her robes
And out she rushed. 'My plague!' I cried. 'So I'm no more worth your
        while?
Have you found a sweeter lapful? Be off and fondle him,
Your other darling. It's for him your tears drop big as apples.'
    When to its young beneath the eaves the swallow has brought home
Some dainty morsel, swiftly it flies off, to seek fresh food:
With speed yet swifter did she run from her soft-cushioned chair
Through vestibule and folding doors, wherever her feet might lead her.
'Off went the bull,' the proverb says, 'and was lost in the wood.'
    Twenty—then eight days—and then nine—and then another ten—
Today's the eleventh—add two more—and there you have two months
Since last we met. I may be Thracian-cropped[1] for aught she knows.
It's all Wolf now: for Wolf the door is left unlocked at night.
But I am not worth reckoning, dropped clean out of account,
Like those wretched Megarians, last and lowest in the list.[2]
If I could leave off loving her, all might go well: but now
How can I? Like the mouse, I've tasted pitch, Thyōnichos.
And what may be the remedy for hopeless love like mine,
I know not; save that Simos, who loved Epichalcos' daughter,
Went overseas and came back cured, a man of just my age.
I too will cross the water, and prove neither the worst,
Nor yet the best may be, but a good average sort of soldier.

[1] The Thracians wore their hair and beard long.
[2] The Megarians, having asked the Delphic oracle which was the noblest city of Greece, were told that Argos was best for soil, Sparta for women, Syracuse for men, etc., but that the Megarians were neither third, nor fourth, nor twelfth, but out of the reckoning altogether.

THYŌNICHOS. Well, Aischines, I could have wished that your desires had
    prospered.
But if in earnest you're resolved to try your luck abroad,
Then Ptolemy[1] of all paymasters for a free man is the best.
AISCHINES. Tell me some more about him.
THYŌNICHOS.   For a free man he's the best:
Kind-hearted, a poet, a true lover, a right good comrade too,
One who can recognise a friend, and a foe better still;
Gives much to many, and when one asks him will refuse no boon
A king may grant: yet it were wise not to be always asking,
Aischines. So if you've a mind to wear your soldier's cloak
Buckled on your right shoulder, and will find the heart to bide,
With both feet planted firm, the brunt of a bold targeteer,
Why then, off straight to Egypt! We're all older than we were;
Our temples show that plain enough: and down from cheek to chin
Steals whitening Time. There's deeds to do, while the knee is nimble yet.

[1] Ptolemy Philadelphus, King of Egypt, who reigned from 287 to 247 B.C.

IDYLL XV

THE SYRACUSAN WOMEN AT THE
ADONIS FESTIVAL

Gorgo and Praxinoa, two young married women, Syracusan by birth, but residing
at Alexandria, set out to see the festival of the Adonis Resurrection in the palace of
Ptolemy Philadelphus. After various adventures in the crowded streets, they at last
squeeze their way in through the palace doors, and there listen to the dainty Resurrection hymn, sung by a professional singing-woman.

GORGO. Praxinoa at home?

PRAXINOA.   Dear Gorgo, at last! Yes, I'm at home.
The wonder is you've come at all. Eunoa, fetch her a chair,
And throw a cushion on it.

GORGO.   Pray, don't trouble.

PRAXINOA.   Do sit down.

GORGO. What a giddy, madcap thing to do! I've scarce got through alive,
Praxinoa, what with all that crowd, and all those four-horsed cars.
Everywhere soldiers' boots, everywhere troopers in fine cloaks!
And the street's endless. Really, my dear, you live too far away.

PRAXINOA. Yes, for that lunatic needs must come to the ends of the earth
        and take
This hole—one can't call it a house—on purpose to prevent
Our being neighbours—all for spite as usual, the jealous wretch!

GORGO. You mustn't say such things, my dear, about your husband Dinon,
When the boy's listening. Do take care. See how he's staring at you!
Never mind, Zopyrion, sweet pet. She doesn't mean papa.

PRAXINOA. By our Lady,[1] the child understands.

GORGO.   Yes, he's a nice papa.

PRAXINOA. The other day that papa of his—yes only the other day
We said, 'Daddy, go to the shop and buy some rouge and soda,'—
Well, back he comes to us with salt, the great thirteen-foot lout!

GORGO. Mine's just the same, that money-swallowing ninny, Diokleides.
He bought five fleeces yesterday at seven drachmas each,
Dogskins, shreds of old wallets, all filth, mere trouble wasted.
But come now, fetch your mantle and your gown and put them on,
Then do let's go to the palace of rich Ptolemy the King,

---

[1] The Goddess Persephone.

To see the Adonis: for I hear this show the Queen's[1] providing
Is quite too lovely.

PRAXINOA.   Oh, of course, all's grand in grand folk's houses.

GORGO. What sights you'll see! What tales to tell to those who haven't seen
    them!
It's time we started.

PRAXINOA.   With idle folk it's always holiday.

She makes up her mind to go

Eunoa, fetch the water, lazy thing, and put it down
Here.—What, asleep again! Those cats just love to be softly dozing.[2]
Come bustle; bring some water quick.—It's water I want first,
And she brings soap.—Well, give it me.—Not so much, you wasteful girl!—
Now pour it out.—You stupid, why d'you spill it on my dress?—
Stop!—There now, I've washed myself as much as the Gods would have me.
Where's the key of the big chest? Find it and bring it here.

GORGO. Praxinoa, that full-bodied gown becomes you mighty well.
Do tell me, what did the stuff cost you when it came off the loom?

PRAXINOA. Ah, don't remind me, Gorgo. More than two good clean minas
Of silver.[3] And besides I put my whole soul in the work.

GORGO. You ought to be pleased with the result.

PRAXINOA.   How nice of you to say so!
Bring me my mantle, girl, and set my hat on stylishly.
No, I don't mean to take *you*, child. Horse-bogies bite little boys.
Yes, cry as much as ever you like; but I can't have you lamed.
Now let's be moving. Phrygia, take the child and play with him;
Call in the dog, and don't forget to bolt the outer door.

They go out into the street

O ye Gods, what a crowd! How are we ever to get through
This dreadful crush? They're swarming thick as ants, endless and countless.
Many indeed are the good turns you've done us, Ptolemy,[4]
Since your sire joined the immortals. No villain comes creeping up
Behind one in the Egyptian style to rob one in the streets—
The sort of games those rascals stuffed with villainy used to play,

---

[1] The Queen was Arsinoe, wife and sister of Ptolemy Philadelphus.
[2] In this passage I have followed Headlam, who reads νίμμα, 'water for washing',
instead of νᾶμα, and puts a colon after θές.
[3] Perhaps about £8.
[4] Ptolemy Soter, the founder of the dynasty, died, and so became a god, 287 B.C.

Birds of a feather, wicked tricksters, scoundrels everyone!—
Sweetest Gorgo! Oh, what *will* become of us! Here they are,
The King's war-horses!—My good man, don't trample on me, please.
Look, that bay's rearing! What a savage brute! Quick, Eunoa, run,
You reckless girl! The beast will kill the man who's leading it.
My goodness, what a blessing that I left the child indoors!

GORGO. Courage, Praxinoa! See, we're safe behind them. They've gone on
And reached their station.

PRAXINOA.   Now I can collect myself again.
A horse and a cold snake are the two things I've dreaded most
Ever since childhood.—Come along quick! There's a huge crowd pouring up.

GORGO (*to an Old Woman*). Do you come from the palace, mother?

OLD WOMAN.   Yes, my dears.

GORGO.   Well, is it easy
To get inside?

OLD WOMAN.   By trying the Greeks got into Troy,
My pretty young lady. If one tries, there's nothing one can't do.

GORGO. Her oracles delivered, away the old wife goes.

PRAXINOA. Women can tell one everything, even how Zeus wedded
    Hera.

GORGO. Just look, Praxinoa, what a crush there is about the doors!

PRAXINOA. Isn't it awful? Gorgo, let me have your hand; and Eunoa,
Catch hold of Eutychis. Mind you hold her tight, or you'll get lost.
Let's all go in together. Stick fast to us, Eunoa.
O dear, what a disaster! There's my summer mantle, Gorgo,
Torn right in two already! For God's sake, my good sir,
As you hope for good fortune, do be careful of my cloak.

STRANGER. I can't do much; but what I can I'll do.

PRAXINOA.   It *is* a crowd.
They're pushing like pigs.

STRANGER.   Courage, madam! We're in a safe place now.

PRAXINOA. And in a safe place may you dwell all your life long, dear sir,
For the way you've taken care of us.—What a kind considerate man!—
Look, there's poor Eunoa getting squeezed.—Come push, you goose! push
    hard!
Good! 'All inside,' as the bridegroom said, when he bolted the door on the
    bride.

GORGO. Praxinoa, do come here. First look at these embroidered stuffs;
How delicate, how lovely! One might call them robes for the Gods.

PRAXINOA. Holy Athana, but what clever weavers must have worked them!
What artists must they be who could design such life-like figures!
How naturally they seem to stand and move, as though alive,
And not mere woven tapestries! Well, man is a cunning creature.
And there, see, on his silver couch he lies, the God himself,
How lovely! with the first soft down just showing on his cheeks,
The thrice-beloved Adonis, even in Acheron beloved.[1]
SECOND STRANGER. Do stop, you tiresome women, your interminable
      chatter,
Like cooing doves. They'll bore me to death with all those broadened vowels.
PRAXINOA. Indeed! Who's this?—What is it, sir, to you, if we *do* chatter?
Order the slaves you've paid for, not Syracusan ladies.
Let me inform you too, we come of good Corinthian stock,[2]
As did Bellerophon. What we talk is Peloponnesian, sir;
And Dorians have the right to speak in Doric, I presume.
Honey-sweet Persephone, may we never know a master,
Save one. I'm not afraid of you, sir, cutting my rations down.
GORGO. Praxinoa, do stop talking; look, the daughter of Argeia
Is going to sing the Adonis. She's a most accomplished artist,
The very same who won the prize for dirge-singing last year.
I warrant we shall hear something fine. She's struck her pose already.
SINGING-WOMAN. Sovereign Goddess, thou who lovest Golgoi, and Idalion,
And lofty Eryx, Aphrodite, thou that playest with gold!
Lo, after twelve months from the eternal stream of Acheron
The softly pacing Hours have brought thee thine Adonis back,
Those tardiest of the blessed Gods, the dear Hours: ah, but desired
They come, for to all living men they ever bring some gift.
Cypris, child of Dione, thou, so is the story told,
From mortal to immortal Berenike[3] didst thou change,
Bedewing her fair bosom with ambrosial drops divine.
And so for thy delight, O thou of many names and shrines,
Doth Berenike's daughter, Arsinoë, fair as Helen,
With all things lovely adorn the couch whereon Adonis slumbers.

---

[1] In a marginal note to these lines Macaulay writes: 'This passage, comic as it is,
indicates the strong sensibility of the whole Greek nation to the beauty of fine works
of art.'
[2] Syracuse was founded by Dorians from Corinth.
[3] Berenike was the wife of Ptolemy I, and became a goddess at some date between
279 and 275 B.C.

Beside him lie ripe fruits of every kind the tall trees bear,
And beside him, set in silver baskets, many a dainty garden,
And Syrian myrrh in alabaster boxes, gold-inlaid.
All pastries such as women mould upon the kneading tray,
Mingling flowers of every sort into white wheaten meal,
Or fashion with sweet honey and soft oil into the shapes
Of every winged and creeping thing, all here are set beside him.
And there green shady arbours with tufts of tender anise
Are built, wherein the little Loves are fluttering overhead,
As on the trees in springtime the youngling nightingales
Make trial of their new-fledged wings, fluttering from bough to bough.
O the ebony! O the gold! O the ivory-carven eagles
That carry to Zeus Kronidas his youthful cupbearer!
And lo the purple carpets spread above, 'softer than sleep,'
So Miletus and the Samian sheep-farmer will say.
For the beautiful Adonis a separate bed is strewn,
One bed for Cypris, and another for rosy-armed Adonis.
The bridegroom is a youth of eighteen summers or nineteen;
His kisses prick not; golden yet is the down upon his lips.
And now farewell to Cypris with her lover in her arms.
But at dawn, while the dew is fresh, together will we come,
And bear him forth to where the waves are plashing on the shore;
And there with loosened locks and robes to the ankles falling down,
With bosoms bared will we begin our clear-voiced threnody.
O loved Adonis, thou alone of demigods, men say,
Dost visit both this world and Acheron's stream. For Agamemnon
Had no such fate, nor Aias, that great hero, wrath-devoured,
Nor Hektor, who was eldest-born of Hekabe's twenty sons,
Not Pátrokles, not Pyrrhos, who came home safe from Troy,
Nor those yet earlier Lapithai, or Deukalion and his sons,
Not Pelops' line, nor the Pelasgian chiefs, the pride of Argos.
Be gracious, loved Adonis, now, and next year too be kind.
Dear has thy coming been, Adonis; dear shall be thy return.
GORGO. Praxinoa, of all creatures the cleverest is woman.
Happy is she to know so much, thrice happy to sing so sweetly.
All the same we must be getting home: Diokleides wants his dinner.
And the man's all vinegar. Don't you venture near him when he's hungry.
Farewell, Adonis darling, and come back to bless us soon.

IDYLL XVI

THE GRACES, OR HIERO

In this poem Theocritus complains of the meanness of the rich, and of their neglect of poets, as compared with the generosity of former ages. He concludes with the praises of Hiero, the champion of the Sicilian Greeks against the Carthaginians and Mamertines, who was then (275 B.C.) the general in chief, and five years later the king of Syracuse. Though he does not make a direct request for Hiero's patronage, he suggests that possibility by graceful hints.

It is ever the care of the Maids of Zeus, ever the care of minstrels,
To hymn the immortal Gods, to hymn the praise of noble heroes.
Goddesses are the Muses, and Goddesses sing of Gods;
But we on earth are mortal men, so of men let us men sing.
   Now who of all that dwell beneath gray dawn, will open his door
And with a kindly welcome receive into his house
My Graces,[1] and not rather send them without gifts away?
So they with frowning visages bare-footed come back home,
And jeer at me because on a fool's errand they were sent;
Then once more listlessly, with heads bowed upon chilly knees,
They sit crouched at the bottom of the empty chest, where still
Is their abode, whenever they return from a bootless quest.
Who now is such? Who will befriend one that speaks well of him?
I know not: for no longer are men eager as of old
To be praised for good deeds, but all by greed of gain are mastered.
Each, with hands hid beneath his gown, spies round, whence he may win
Money; nor even the rust of it would he rub off for a gift,
But has his proverbs ready: 'The shin is further than the knee.
First something for myself! 'Tis for the Gods to honour minstrels.
Who wants to listen to another? Homer's enough for all.
He is the best of minstrels who gets nothing out of me.'
   Good sirs, what profit is there in uncounted hoards of gold?
Not such for the wise is the true fruit of wealth; but to bestow
On your own soul a part thereof, part haply upon some minstrel;
To benefit many a kinsman, and many a man besides,
And ceaselessly to sacrifice at the altars of the Gods;
Never to be a churlish host, but generously entreat

---

[1] By 'my Graces' Theocritus means his poems.

And speed the guest, when he would fain depart; but above all
To honour the sacred prophets of the Muses, that so, even
When you lie hidden in Hades, a fair fame you may win,
Nor roam without renown beside Acheron's chilly stream,
Like one whose palms are hardened by the spade, some needy son
Of needy parents, wailing his landless poverty.

Many once were the bondmen, who earned their monthly dole
Within the halls of king Aleuas and Antiochos;[1]
Many the calves that to the byres of the Skopadai
Were driven lowing homeward, among the horned kine;
And countless upon Krannon's plain were the sheep of choice breed
Pastured by the shepherds of the hospitable Kreondai.
Yet no joy had these lords therefrom, once into the wide barge
Of that abhorred old boatman[2] they had breathed sweet life away,
But unremembered, though they had left behind them all that wealth,
Would they have lain for evermore among the unhonoured dead,
Had not the glorious Keian minstrel, uttering varied song
To his lyre of many strings, bestowed fame on them among men
Unborn, and had they never won renown by their swift steeds,
That came home to them crowned with victory from the sacred games.
And who of the Lycian princes, who of Priam's long-haired sons
Had ever known, or of Kuknos, as a woman white of skin,
If minstrels had not hymned the battles of those men of old?
And Odysseus, though he wandered among all the tribes of men
For six times twenty months, and while yet living visited
Uttermost Hades, and escaped the murderous Cyclops' cave,
No lasting glory had he won, and silent would have been
The names of swineherd Eumaios, and of Philoitios
Herdsman of kine, and even of Laertes great of heart,
Unless the Ionian with his songs had blessed their memory.

Verily from the Muses comes fair renown to men:
Yet when they are dead, their wealth is wasted by their living heirs.
But sure it were as easy to stand on the beach and count
How many waves the wind drives shoreward over the blue sea,
Or in clear water to wash clean a dirty brick of mud,
As to win favour from a man smitten with lust of gain.

[1] Aleuas, Antiochos, the Skopadai and the Kreondai were princes or nobles of
Thessaly, and patrons of Simonides, the Keian minstrel, who lived from 556 to 467 B.C.
[2] Charon, the ferryman of the dead.

Farewell to such. May silver beyond reckoning be his,
And may a craving for more riches ever possess his soul.
But for myself, honour and friendship from my fellow-men
I'ld rather choose, before much wealth in horses and in mules.

    Now would I seek to whom of mortals, as a welcome guest
Led by the Muses, I may come; for hard are the roads to minstrels
Without the escort of those daughters of deep-counselling Zeus.
Not yet of driving onward the months and years has Heaven
Grown weary, and oft shall the Sun's horses speed the car of Day,
And the man who shall require me as his minstrel shall be found,
When he has wrought such deeds as great Achilles or dread Aias
Wrought in the plains of Simoïs, where is Phrygian Ilos' tomb.

    Already the Phoenicians, who beneath the setting sun
Dwell on the spur of Libya,[1] are shuddering for fear.
Already the Syracusans are gripping their spears firm,
And each man with a wicker shield is burdening his arm;
And Hiero among them, like a hero of old times,
Girds himself, while a horse-hair plume is shadowing his helm.
O thou most glorious Father Zeus, and thou, holy Athene,
And thou, Maiden, who with thy Mother guardest the great burg
Of the wealthy Ephyraians,[2] by Lysimeleia's stream,
Now may defeat drive forth our foes from the island, carrying home
The tidings of their dear ones' death o'er the Sardinian waves
To wives and children, a scanty remnant of so great a host.
But all our towns that hostile hands have utterly laid waste,
May they be once more dwelt in by their former citizens;
And once more may our fertile fields be tilled, and may our sheep,
Fattening in countless thousands mid the herbage, o'er the plains
Roam bleating; while great droves of cattle, homing to their stalls,
Warn the twilight traveller to hasten on his way;
May fallows be ploughed up against the seed-time, while cicalas,
Watching the shepherds toiling in the sun, sing from the twigs
Of tree-tops; and may spiders over shield and helmet weave
Their frail webs, and no talk be heard of the war-cry any more.
But Hiero's fame let minstrels waft on high, northward across
The Scythian sea, and eastward to where reigned Semiramis,

    [1] The Carthaginians.
    [2] The Maiden and her Mother are Persephone and Demeter. Ephyra was the ancient name of Corinth, of which Syracuse was a colony.

She who built the broad wall and with asphalt bound it fast.[1]
I am but one of many whom the daughters of Zeus love;
And all of them delight to sing Sicilian Arethusa,
And the people of her city, and valiant Hiero.

O divine Graces, first adored by Eteokles![2] O lovers
Of Minyan Orchomenos, that ancient foe of Thebes!
If none invite me, at home will I abide; but to the house
Of such as bid me, boldly with my Muses will I come.
You too I'll bring: for what without the Graces can men know
Desirable? With the Graces evermore may I dwell!

[1] The Greeks supposed Babylon to have been built by a mythical queen called
Semiramis.

[2] Eteokles, a legendary king of Orchomenos in Boeotia, was said to have been the
first to offer sacrifice to the Graces.

IDYLL XVII

AN ENCOMIUM OF PTOLEMY

This panegyric of Ptolemy Philadelphus was probably written at Alexandria about
273 B.C. It is to the credit of Theocritus that he is not at his best when required to
write a poem of this kind. Yet insincere and artificial as it may be, there are few pieces
of poetic flattery that are less tedious to read, or that are redeemed by so many fine
lines.

WITH Zeus let us begin, ye Muses, and be our ending Zeus,
Whene'er we celebrate in song the noblest of the Gods.
But of men first and foremost let Ptolemy be named,
And last, and midst; for among men he is pre-eminent.
The heroes who in olden days of demigods were born
Found cunning minstrels to make known the valiant deeds they wrought:
And so I, who am skilful in shapely song, would fain
Hymn Ptolemy; for hymns bring honour even to the Gods.
When a woodman has come up to Ida's forest, he peers round
Wondering, among so many trees, where to begin his task.
And I, of what first shall I tell? For countless are the ways,
Wherein the Gods have honoured this noblest among kings.

  By virtue of his sires, how apt to achieve his mighty work
Was Ptolemy, Lagus' son, when once he had stored within his mind
Such a design as no man else had power to conceive!
Him has the Father stablished in equal honour now
With the blessed Gods; and in the house of Zeus for him is built
A golden mansion; and by his side sits Alexander throned,
His loving friend, a grievous God to the bright-tiara'd Persians.
Over against them there is set the throne of Herakles,
The slayer of the Centaurs, wrought of stubborn adamant,
Where feasting blissfully he sits with the other sons of Heaven,
Rejoicing in his children's children with exceeding joy,
Because Kronidas from their limbs has purged old age away,
And now they are called immortal Gods, since they were born his offspring.
For the strong son of Herakles to both is ancestor,[1]
And both reckon their lineage back to Herakles at last.

---

[1] By 'the strong son of Herakles' is probably meant his descendant Karānos, who
founded the Macedonian dynasty in the eighth century B.C., and was the ancestor both
of Alexander and Ptolemy.

Therefore when now of fragrant nectar he has drunk his fill,
And from the feast would fain depart to the house of his dear wife,
To one he gives his bow and quiver that hangs beneath his elbow,
To the other his great club, jagged with knots, more hard than iron.
So they to the ambrosial bower of the white-ankled Hebe
Carry his weapons, and escort the bearded son of Zeus.

Again, how gloriously shone forth illustrious Berenike
Among wise women, a proud joy to these that gave her birth!
Her fragrant bosom did the holy daughter of Dione,
Who hath her shrine in Cyprus' isle, stroke with her slender hands:
Therefore, they say, no woman ever gave delight to man
So great as Ptolemy received from the love he bore his wife.
Aye, with a love far greater was he loved again: and thus
Securely may a husband trust his whole house to his children,
When to the bed he goes of one who loves him as he doth her.
But a wife who loves not, ever sets her mind on some strange man.
Children she bears in plenty; but none are like the father.
Queen Aphrodite, thou the first in beauty of Goddesses,
Thy care was she; and by thy favour lovely Berenike
O'er Acheron, the stream of lamentation, never passed,
But away didst thou snatch her, ere she came to the dark ship,
And the ever-hateful ferryman of the dead, and in thy shrine
Didst throne her, and of thy worship bestow on her a share.
So now into all mortals with kindly power she breathes
Soft longings, and makes light the cares of him that pines for love.

O dark-browed Argive princess, thou, that wert Tydeus' bride,
Didst bear man-slaying Diomed, the hero of Calydon;
Likewise deep-girded Thetis to Aiakid Peleus bare
Spearman Achilles; and so thee, thou warrior Ptolemy,
To Ptolemy the warrior bare the glorious Berenike.
Then did Kos from thy mother's hand receive thee, a new-born babe,
And cherish thee, that hour when first thou didst behold the dawn.
For there Antigone's daughter cried aloud on Eileithyia,[1]
The loosener of the girdle, in her bitter childbirth pangs;
And the Goddess came to comfort her, and over all her limbs
Shed down release from pain. So in the likeness of his sire
A beloved boy was born. Then Kos, when she beheld, cried out

---

[1] Eileithyia was the goddess of child-birth. Ptolemy Philadelphus was born in the island of Kos.

For rapture, and in loving hands clasping the babe, spoke thus:
'Blessed mayest thou be, O child! and mayest thou honour me
No less than Phoebus Apollo honours azure-crownèd Delos!
And stablish in the same renown the hill of Triopon,[1]
Assigning equal privilege to the Dorians who dwell near,
Even as king Apollo loveth Rhenaia's rock.'
So spoke the isle; and from on high out of the clouds there came
The scream of a great eagle, thrice, a fortunate augury.
From Zeus, I ween, was this a sign. Revered kings are the wards
Of Zeus the son of Kronos. But that king is supreme,
Whom Zeus hath loved even from his birth. Great fortune is ever his:
O'er many lands he hath dominion, and o'er many seas.

A myriad countries are there, and a myriad tribes of men,
Which bring forth harvests ripening beneath the rain of Zeus:
Yet no land beareth crops so rich as Egypt's level plain,
When Nile with overflowing flood soaks and breaks up the soil.
No land else hath so many towns where skilful craftsmen dwell.
Therein of cities builded there stand three centuries,
And thousands three, and yet again three tens of thousands more,
Then twice three cities, and beside all these yet three times nine:[2]
In every one the noble-hearted Ptolemy reigns as king.
Aye, and he claims his portion of Phoenicia and Arabia,
Of Syria, Libya, and the land of the black Aethiops.
Over Cilicia's spearmen and the Pamphylians all
He rules, and o'er the Lycians, and the war-loving Karians,
And the islands of the Cyclades; since his are the best ships
That sail on the deep waters. Thus do all those seas and lands
And sounding rivers own the sway of Ptolemy the king.
Many too are the horsemen, many the targeteers
That gather round his standard harnessed in gleaming bronze.
In treasure he outweighs all other kings; such mighty wealth
To his rich palace day by day pours in from every side;
While in security his people go about their labours.
For here no foeman, marching o'er the monster-teeming Nile,
Has raised the cry of battle among townships not his own;
Nor yet have mail-clad raiders from their swift ships leapt forth
On the sea-beach of Egypt to make havoc of her herds;

[1] Triopon was a promontory in Karia; Rhenaia was a small rocky island near Delos.
[2] $300+3000+30000+3+3+3^3=33333$, a mystic number.

So mighty is the hero who sits throned in these broad plains,
Even the fair-haired Ptolemy, well-skilled to wield the spear,
Whose chiefest care is to preserve the heritage of his sires,
As a good king should; and somewhat more he adds thereto himself.
And yet not idle and useless in his opulent house the gold
Lies heaped together like the wealth of ever-toiling ants.
But the illustrious temples of the Gods have their full share,
Since evermore he renders them first-fruits, with other dues.
Moreover much he lavishes in gifts to mighty kings,
Much he bestows on cities, much upon faithful friends.
And to the sacred contests at the feasts of Dionysus
Comes no man having skill to lift his voice in tuneful song,
Whom he rewards not with some gift worthy of the minstrel's art.
In gratitude for such benefits the prophets of the Muses
Sing Ptolemy's praise. And what more glorious destiny can there be
For him who is prosperous, than to earn a fair fame among men?
This it is that abideth still with Atreus' sons; but all
That countless spoil they won, when Priam's mighty house they stormed,
Lies hidden somewhere in that mist whence there is no return.

 Alone of all the men of elder ages, or of those
Whose yet warm steps are printed in the dust they trod, this man
Hath built shrines sweet with incense to his sire and mother dear;
And therein hath he set their statues, all adorned with gold
And ivory, to be saviours of all men who dwell on earth.
And there on the empurpled altars, as the months come round,
Many are the fat thighs of kine he burns in sacrifice,
He and his noble queen, than whom a wife more virtuous
Never yet cast her arms around a bridegroom in her bower;
For with her whole heart doth she love her brother and her spouse.
Such were the holy nuptials too of those immortal Gods
Whom mighty Rhea bare to be the rulers of Olympus:
And one couch for the slumber of Hera and of Zeus
Doth the still-virgin Iris strew with myrrh-anointed hands.

 Farewell, lord Ptolemy. Thee, no less than the other demigods,
My song shall praise. And this my word, methinks, men yet unborn
Will not reject: 'For righteousness, make thou thy prayer to Zeus.'

IDYLL XVIII

AN EPITHALAMIUM FOR HELEN

This is an epithalamium for the marriage of Menelaos and Helen, sung by a chorus
of twelve Spartan maidens before the doors of the bridal chamber. The Scholiast says
that Theocritus is here imitating a lost epithalamium for Helen by Stesichorus, the
great Sicilian lyric poet of the sixth century. It is interesting to compare this poem
with the fragments of Sappho's marriage songs, and with Catullus LXII.

In Sparta once, within the halls of golden-haired Menelaos,
Twelve maidens, their tresses wreathed with flowering hyacinth,
The city's pride, the glory of Laconian womanhood,
Before the newly painted chamber set their dance in order,
When Atreus' younger son had wooed and won the lovely Helen,
Daughter of Tyndarus, and shut the bridal bower's door.
Then they all sang together to one tune, beating time
With woven paces, while the house rang with the nuptial hymn.

'Can it be thou art slumbering thus early, bridegroom dear?
With heaviness are thy limbs weighed down? Of sleep art thou so fond?
Or perchance hast thou drunk too deep and flung thee on thy bed?
If thou wast fain to sleep betimes, thou shouldst have slept alone,
And left the maiden with her maidens by her fond mother's side
To play till dawn is spreading, since tomorrow and next day,
Menelaos, and for all years to come henceforth she is thy bride.

O happy bridegroom, someone sneezed good fortune on thy quest,
As with the other princes thou wast journeying to Sparta.
Alone among the demigods shalt thou have Zeus for father:
Beneath one coverlet with thee the daughter of Zeus hath come,
Whose peer among Achaian maidens treadeth not the earth.
Should the child be like its mother, sure a marvel would she bear.
All we were of like age with her; the same races we ran,
Anointed in manly fashion beside Eurotas' streams,
Four times sixty girls, the maiden flower of the land:
Yet of us all there would be none found faultless, matched with Helen.

Beautiful is the countenance that rising Dawn shows forth;
Fair is the holy Night, and gleaming Spring when Winter wanes;
So among us in her beauty doth golden Helen shine.
To rich ploughed lands a glory doth a mighty harvest spring,
A cypress to the garden, a horse of Thessaly to the car;

Even so is rose-red Helen our Lacedaemon's pride.
No other from her basket spins such fine threads of wool,
And none from the tall beams can cut a closer warp away
Than that which with her shuttle in the carven loom she weaves.
Yea, and none other hath such skill to strike the lyre's strings,
Hymning the praise of Artemis and broad-breasted Athene,
As Helen, she within whose eyes inhabit all the Loves.

O fair, O gracious damsel, a housewife art thou now.
But we at dawn to the race-course and to the flowering meads
Will hasten, there to pluck and twine sweet-breathing coronals;
And often longingly on thee, dear Helen, shall we think,
As tender lambs yearn for the teat of the ewe that gave them birth.
A garland of earth-creeping lotus we will be the first
To wreathe for thee, and hang it on a shady plane-tree's boughs;
And we first from a silver phial of soft-flowing oil
Upon the shady plane-tree's roots will pour it drop by drop.
And letters on the bark in Dorian wise shall be engraved,
That passers-by may read: "Worship me: I am Helen's tree."

Farewell, O bride! Farewell, thou groom, who hast won a sire divine!
May Leto, fostering nurse of noble sons, may Leto bring you
Fair offspring; Cypris, holy Cypris grant you equal joys
In love; and Zeus, Kronos-born Zeus, imperishable wealth,
And endless heritage from princely sire to princely son.
Sleep then, breathing upon the breast each of the other love
And love's desire; but with the dawn forget not to awake.
For in the morning will we come, soon as the earliest cock
Shrills from his perch, outstretching his feathery neck to crow.

Hymen, O Hymenaios, in this bridal take thou joy!'

IDYLL XIX

THE HONEY-STEALER

Nothing can be said with certainty about the authorship and date of this elegant trifle, except that it is not by Theocritus, nor by any poet of his period. There is a well-known imitation of this poem among the Anacreontics, which were probably written in Byzantine times.

ONCE did a wicked bee sting thievish Love
While he was pilfering honeycomb from a hive,
And pricked his finger-tips. Feeling the pain,
He blew on his hand and stamped upon the ground
And jumped about, then came and showed his hurt
To Aphrodite, and weeping made complaint
How that the bee is such a tiny beast,
Yet what great wounds it makes! But his mother laughed
And said, 'Why, silly boy, are you not just
Like to the bees yourself, since you are such
A tiny thing, yet can make such great wounds?'

IDYLL XX

THE YOUNG COWMAN

This amusing and spirited poem is certainly not by Theocritus, but perhaps by some
early imitator. The grounds upon which scholars have rejected it are linguistic and
metrical, and so are concealed by translation; but the poem is also full of obvious
verbal echoes of Theocritus, whereas in style, movement and tone it is quite different.

EUNIKA mocked me, when I fain had given her a sweet kiss,
And railing at me, thus she spoke: 'Go with a mischief, go!
Wretch, would you kiss me, you a cowherd? Never have I learnt
To kiss in country fashion, but to press town-bred lips.
I will not have you kiss my lovely mouth, not even in dreams.
Oh, how you look and how you talk! How boorish is your play!
How wantonly you wheedle me! How glibly you discourse!
And then your beard, how soft it is! How fragrant smells your hair!
Your lips are all beslobbered, and your hands are black with filth,
And you smell rank. Begone, lest you befoul me with your touch.'
These words she spoke, then thrice into her bosom did she spit,[1]
All the time staring at me from my head down to my feet
With scornfully pouting lips and eyes that leered at me askance,
While wantonly she swayed her body, laughing in my face
An impudent disdainful laugh, till suddenly my blood boiled,
And I grew crimson beneath the sting, like a rose drenched with dew.
So away she flung and left me there. But it rankles in my heart
That a vile whore should flout and mock a handsome man like me.
　　Shepherds, tell me the very truth: am I not beautiful?
Has some God changed me suddenly into a different man?
For round me till this hour there bloomed a winsome comeliness,
Like ivy about a tree-stem, and adorned my cheek and chin;
And round my temples curling like parsley fell my locks,
And over my black eyebrows white and fair my forehead gleamed,
While far more brightly shone these eyes than the bright glance of Athene;
Aye, and sweeter were my lips than cream-cheese, and therefrom
My voice would flow forth sweeter than honey from the comb.
Sweet is my music too, whether I warble on the pipe,
Or discourse on the flute, or on the reed or flageolet.

[1] The Greeks spat in order to avert the evil eye (cp. Idyll VI, 39).

Then all the maidens on the hills tell me that I am comely,
And they all give me kisses; yet this town-wench would not kiss me,
But because I am a cowherd, ran away and will not hear me.
Did not fair Dionysus drive heifers through the glens?
And knows she not how Cypris for a herdsman was distraught,
And tended cattle on the Phrygian mountains? In the woods
Did she not love, and in the woods bewail Adonis dead?
Who was Endymion? Was he not a cowherd? Yet the Moon
Loved him as he was pasturing his herd, and from Olympus
Came down, and stealing through the grove, slept one sleep with the lad.
Thou, Rhea, weepest for thy neatherd.[1] Thou too, Kronidas,
Didst thou not wander as a bird to win a cowboy's love?
But alone Eunika would not love a herdsman, and thereby
Than Cybele she is greater, and than Cypris, and Selene.
Nevermore, Cypris, may she hold her darling in her arms,
Whether in town or on the hills, but sleep all night alone.

[1] Rhea, or Cybele, the mother of Zeus, loved the shepherd Atys; and Zeus, according to one version of the legend, changed himself into an eagle in order to carry off Ganymede.

IDYLL XXI

THE FISHERMEN

Two poor fishermen are lying awake by night in their cabin by the sea. Asphalion has just dreamt that he has been catching a marvellous golden fish. Being troubled by the promise he has made in his dream, never again to set foot on the sea, he asks the advice of his companion, who reassures him: he has not sworn, any more than he has caught the golden fish.

The text is unusually corrupt, and in several passages the true reading is very doubtful.

This Idyll is considered by most scholars not to be the work of Theocritus. Probably it is by Leonidas of Tarentum, his contemporary, or at least by an imitator of that poet. It is perhaps natural, though hardly reasonable, to be impatient of the criticism which takes away so beautiful a masterpiece from a great master, and assigns it to an obscure writer. Yet it detracts nothing from our enjoyment of an anonymous ballad, such as *Helen of Kirconnell*, that we know nothing of its author. These questions are bound to seem of greater importance to the scholars who have to deal with them, than to us who are content merely to enjoy the poems.

It is Poverty, Diophantos, that alone can rouse the crafts.
Labour's schoolmistress is she. For men who live by toil
May not so much as slumber because of cruel cares.
Nay, if for a brief while at night he close his eyes, forthwith
Troubles come thronging round him and disquieting his sleep.

    Two aged fishermen one night were lying side by side
On beds of dry sea-tangle within their wattled huts,
Leaning against a wall of leafy boughs, and round about
Lay strewn those implements of their toiling hands, their wicker creels
And rods of reed, their fishing hooks, their ground-baits of seaweed,
Lines and weels and lobster-pots woven with cords of rush,
Seines and a pair of oars and an old cobble upon props.
Beneath their heads lay a scanty matting: for rugs they had their coats.
Such for these fishers was their whole equipment, their whole wealth.
Key, door and watchdog they had none: to them such things seemed all
Superfluous; for Poverty was their faithful sentinel.
Close at hand dwelt no neighbour; but with gentle plashing waves
Around their narrow cabin came floating up the sea.

    Not yet had the Moon's chariot reached the mid-point of her course,
When their familiar toil awaked those fishers. From their eyes
They thrust out slumber, and their thoughts broke forth into speech thus.

ASPHALION. They speak not true, my friend, all those who tell us that the nights
Grow shorter in the summer time, when Zeus brings the long days.
Already I've seen ten thousand dreams, and the dawn is not yet come.
Am I wrong? What is happening? How endless the nights seem!
FRIEND. Asphalion, blame you the fair Summer? It is not that the season
Has wilfully overstepped his wonted course; but it is care
That cutting short your slumbers, makes the night seem long to you.
ASPHALION. Did you ever learn to interpret dreams? For it's good ones I've been seeing.
And I'ld not have you miss your share in any vision of mine.
FRIEND. Aye, as we go shares in our catch, so too in all our dreams.
Well, when I guess, I'll make use of my mind. Sure, he should be
The best interpreter of dreams, whose teacher is his mind.
Moreover we have time to spare: for what else can one do,
Thus lying on a leaf-bed by the sea-wave and not sleeping?
Nay, 'tis the donkey among thorns, the lamp in the town-hall;
For these, men say, are always sleepless. Come then, let me hear
Your vision of the night; for friend should tell his dreams to friend.
ASPHALION. Last night when I had fallen asleep, wearied with our sea-toils,
(Though not through over-feeding, for 'twas early we had supped,
Sparing our bellies, as you'll call to mind), I saw myself
Sitting upon a rock and watching eagerly for fish,
While with my rod I jerked and dangled the beguiling bait.
Suddenly something, a fine fat one, nibbled: for in dreams
As every hound surmises a bear, so I a fish.
The hook it seemed had caught him firmly, for the blood was flowing.
My rod was bent all double, so strongly did he pull,
As with both hands I strained it to the breaking: a big struggle
It was to land so great a fish with tackle all too weak.
Then to remind him of his wound, I gave him a gentle prick,
Pricked him, and slackened; then, as he did not bolt, tightened the line.
Now had I won the victory; I drew up a golden fish,
With gold plated all over. But dread took hold of me
Lest he might prove to be some fish by Poseidon beloved,
Or else perchance some jewel prized by green-haired Amphitrite.
So carefully and gently from the hook I loosened him,
For fear the barbs should tear away some gold out of his mouth.
Well, having him, I trusted to live happily on land,

And swore that I would never again set foot upon the sea,
But stay on land and live there with my gold like any king.
This thought awakened me. But now exert your wits, my friend,
To help me: for I am afeard about that oath I swore.
FRIEND. Nay, have no fear. You have not sworn, any more than you caught
That gold-fish you imagined. Your vision was but lies,
A mere hope born of slumber. Seek for the fish of flesh:
For if you still go hunting such vain phantoms in sleep,
Well might you die of hunger and of your golden dreams.

IDYLL XXII

A HYMN TO THE DIOSKURI

This is an epic Hymn, in the Homeric manner, to Kastor and Polydeukes, the twin sons of Zeus, deemed to be the sons of Tyndarus, the husband of their mother, Leda. The first section relates an episode of their voyage on Jason's Argo, the boxing-match between Polydeukes and Amykos, the brutal chieftain of the Bebrykes; the second part tells how Kastor slew Lynkeus in an adventure that was scarcely to the credit of the Great Twin Brethren.

W E hymn the two sons of Leda and of aegis-bearing Zeus, Kastor and Polydeukes, that boxer so formidable to confront, when he has harnessed his hands with the ox-hide thongs. Twice, yea thrice do we hymn the stalwart children of Thestios' daughter, the two Lacedaemonian brethren, those saviours of men who stand upon the very edge of peril, and of horses panic-stricken in the bloody fray, and of ships that defying the stars as they set and rise into the heavens have encountered grievous storm-blasts, which, raising huge surges around the stern, or at the prow, or from whatever quarter they will, fling them into the vessel's hold, shattering both bulwarks, while the sail and all its tackle hang torn and dishevelled, and a great rain falls from the sky as night creeps on, and the wide sea resounds, scourged by the gusts and by the implacable hail. Nevertheless you draw the ships forth from the gulf with their sailors, who had thought themselves dead men, and on a sudden the winds sink down still, and there is an oily calm over all the sea, and this way and that the clouds scatter apart, till the Bears shine forth, and between the Asses dimly peeps out the Manger, betokening that all is fair and smooth for voyaging. O ye helpers of mortal men! O beloved pair, horsemen and harpers, athletes and minstrels! Of Kastor first or of Polydeukes shall I sing? Both will I hymn; but first of Polydeukes shall be my song.

Already had Argo passed safely between the Clashing Rocks, and through the grim mouth of the snowy Pontic sea, and was come to the land of the Bebrykes, carrying on board her the dear children of the Gods. There the men disembarked from either side of Jason's ship, many down one ladder, and landing on the deep sand of a wind-sheltered beach they strewed their beds and rubbed sticks together to make fire. Now Kastor of the fleet steeds and ruddy Polydeukes went both wandering alone, apart from their comrades, gazing at all the various wild-wood trees upon the hills; and beneath a smooth rock they found an ever-flowing spring, brimming with pure clear water, and the pebbles gleamed up from its deep bottom like crystal and silver, while all around grew tall firs, and poplars, and plane-trees, and tapering cypresses, and fragrant flowers, wherein the hairy bees love to labour, such as blossom all over the meadows when spring is waning. And there a monster of a man was sitting sunning himself, terrible to look upon, with his ears crushed by hard bruising blows. His giant breast and his broad back bulged with iron flesh like some hammered statue; and the muscles upon his sturdy arms stood out beneath the shoulder like rounded stones that a wintry stream has rolled and polished in its mighty eddies; while around his back and neck there hung a lion-skin fastened by the claws. To him first spoke the champion Polydeukes.

POLYDEUKES. Good day to you, stranger, whoever you may be. What men are they who dwell in this land?

AMYKOS. How 'good day,' when I see men whom I never set eyes on before?

POLYDEUKES. Be of good cheer. Trust me, we are neither evil men, nor men of an evil stock.

AMYKOS. Of good cheer I am: and it is not for you to teach me that.

POLYDEUKES. Are you a man of the wilds, who takes offence at everything, or a mere vainglorious fellow?

AMYKOS. I'm what you see: and at least I'm not trespassing on your ground.

POLYDEUKES. Come, taste of my hospitality, and then go back home.

AMYKOS. None of your hospitality for me. I've none here ready for you.

POLYDEUKES. My good sir, will you not even allow us to drink of this water?

AMYKOS. That you shall find out when thirst parches your shrivelled lips.

POLYDEUKES. Say, with what may we buy your leave; with silver, or how else?

AMYKOS. Put up your hands and fight it out with me, man to man.

POLYDEUKES. With fists only, or kicking and tripping as well? But eye to eye were best.

AMYKOS. Use your fists and your whole strength too, and don't be sparing of your skill.

POLYDEUKES. And who is it against whom I am to bind the thongs round my hands?

AMYKOS. You see him before you, a boxer whom no one shall call a weakling girl.

POLYDEUKES. But is there a prize ready for us two to fight for?

AMYKOS. I will be called your man, if you win, or you mine.

POLYDEUKES. Such are the battle-cries of red-crested game-cocks.

AMYKOS. Well, whether we be like game-birds, or like lions, we'll fight for no other prize.

So spoke Amykos, and took his hollow shell and sounded it, and quickly at the blowing of the shell the long-haired Bebrykes gathered together under the shady plane-tree; while the peerless warrior Kastor went to summon all the heroes from the Magnesian ship. So the two champions, when they had strengthened their hands with ox-hide thongs, and had twisted the long straps around their arms, met together in the ring, breathing slaughter against each other.

And first they both had much ado, striving eagerly which should get the sun's light at his back. But by thy skill, O Polydeukes, thou didst outwit the big man, so that the beams fell full into the face of Amykos. So he in angry mood pressed forward, sparring; but as he came on, the son of Tyndarus hit him on the tip of his chin, so that he became yet more furious than before, and took to fighting wildly, lunging with his whole weight, and with head bent down. At this the Bebrykes raised a glad cry, while on the other side the heroes thought to hearten stalwart Polydeukes with their shouting, for they feared lest the weight of this great Tityos of a man might crush him and vanquish him in so narrow a ring. But the son of Zeus stood up to him, shifting hither and thither, and kept hitting him with both fists, till he checked the onset of the son of Poseidon, for all his overbearing strength, so that he stood dizzied with the blows, spitting out red blood; and the Greek chieftains all shouted together for joy, when they marked the grievous bruises about his mouth and jaws, and how his eyes were closing up, as his face swelled. Then did the prince bewilder him by feinting at him from every side; but so soon as he saw that Amykos was at his wits' end, he drove with his fist just above the middle of the nose beneath the eyebrows, and laid bare his face to the bone; and this blow stretched him out on his back among the blossoming flowers. When he rose up, the grim fight was renewed, each punishing and bruising the other with the cruel thongs. But while the chieftain of the Bebrykes was ever at work with his fists upon the breast and outside the neck, unconquerable Polydeukes kept pounding his foe's face with ugly blows. The flesh of the one began to melt away in sweat, till he seemed to be quickly shrinking from a mighty man to a little one; but the limbs of the other waxed ever stouter, and his colour better as he settled down to his work.

How then at length did the son of Zeus overthrow that gluttonous fellow? Say, Goddess, for thou knowest; and I, who am but the mouthpiece of others, will speak all that thou wilt, and in such wise as seems good to thee.

And now, in his eagerness to bring off some great stroke, Amykos seized with his left hand the left wrist of Polydeukes, swerving sideways from his guard, then, attacking with his other hand, swung round his broad forearm from his right flank. And had this blow gone home, it would have done grievous harm to the king of Amyklae; but he, ducking his head, came up from beneath, and with his strong right hand struck Amykos on the left temple with the whole force of his shoulder. Swiftly gushed the dark blood from the gaping brow, while with his left he smote his foe's mouth, so that every tooth in it rattled. Then with ever swifter blows did he maul his face, until both cheeks were well pounded. At last he fell full length on the ground and lay there swooning, and held up both his hands to cry off the battle, for he was near to death. Yet thou, O boxer Polydeukes, for all thy victory, didst do him no savage hurt; but he swore to thee a mighty oath, calling upon his father Poseidon to hearken from the deep sea, that never again would he behave brutally to strangers.

Thus have I hymned thy praise, great prince: and now of thee, Kastor, will I sing, thou son of Tyndarus, rider of swift steeds, bronze-corsleted brandisher of the spear.

Now the two sons of Zeus had seized and were carrying away the two daughters of Leukippos; and impetuously pursuing them were their betrothed bridegrooms, those two brethren, the sons of Aphareus, Lynkeus and valiant Idas. But when they came to the tomb of Aphareus, together they all leapt from their chariots, and rushed upon each other, cumbered by the weight of their spears and hollow shields. Then spoke Lynkeus, shouting loudly from beneath his helmet: 'Ye foolish men, wherefore do you desire battle? And how comes it you are so ungentle as to rob others of their brides, with swords naked in your hands? To us did Leukippos betroth these daughters of his, long before you laid claim to them. To us this bridal is confirmed by oath. But you, to win the brides of others, perverted him in unseemly fashion by gifts of oxen and mules and other wealth, and so stole wedlock by bribes. Yet often in the face of you both thus did I speak, though I am not a man of many words: "Not so, good friends, does it become princes to woo wives, who already have bridegrooms betrothed. A wide land is Sparta, and wide is Elis, the country of horses, and Arcadia, rich in sheep, and the cities of the Achaians; wide too is Messene, and Argos, and the sea-coast of Sisyphus.[1] Therein dwell countless maidens, nurtured by the care of their parents, lacking neither in beauty nor in wit; and of these you may easily espouse whomsoever you have a mind to; for there are many would be willing to be fathers-in-law to noble husbands; and you are the very pick and flower of all heroes, you and your fathers, and all the blood of your fathers from of old. Nay, friends, suffer this bridal of ours to come to fulfilment; and for you let all of us devise

[1] Sisyphus was a legendary king of Corinth.

some other marriage." Thus would I often speak; but the wind's breath ever carried my words away over the wet sea-wave; for inexorable and ruthless are you both. Nay, yet even now be persuaded; for you are our cousins by the father's side. But if your hearts are lusting for war, if, stirring up kindred strife, we must bathe our spears in blood, then shall Idas and my kinsman, mighty Polydeukes, draw back their hands from the hateful fray; but let us two, Kastor and I, bring our quarrel to the test of war, we who are the younger born, and so leave the less grief to those who begat us. Enough is one man slain out of one house. But the others shall together feast their friends, and be bridegrooms, not slain men, and shall take these maidens to wife. In truth it were well to settle a great dispute with as little loss as may be.'

So he spoke, and his words the Gods made not vain; for the two elder took their armour from their shoulders and laid it on the ground; but Lynkeus came forward into the midst, shaking his strong lance beneath the rim of his shield; and in like manner Kastor vibrated the point of his spear, while the plumes nodded upon the crests of each. First they made play with their lances, thrusting at one another, if perchance they might espy some spot unguarded. But before either was wounded, the spear-points were broken off, stuck fast in the mighty shields. Then each one drew his sword from his sheath, and again devised the other's death, nor was there any respite from the fight. Many a blow did Kastor deal on his foe's broad shield and horsehair crest; and many a time did keen-eyed Lynkeus dint the shield of Kastor, and his blade just reached the scarlet plume. Then Lynkeus made a cut with his sharp sword at Kastor's left knee, but Kastor drew back his left foot and slashed off the fingers from his foe's right hand, so that he dropped his weapon and rushed in swift flight towards his father's tomb, where mighty Idas lay watching this duel between kinsmen. But the son of Tyndarus darted after him and thrust his broad sword clean through flank and navel, so that the bronze clove the bowels within. Then Lynkeus bowed and lay there fallen on his face, and heavy sleep rushed down upon his eyelids. Nor yet that other child of hers was Laocoösa to behold a happy bridegroom by the hearth of his fathers; for now Messenian Idas, tearing away the grave-stone from the tomb of Aphareus, would have hurled it at the slayer of his brother, had not Zeus come to Kastor's aid, and striking the carved marble from his foe's hands, utterly consumed him with a flaming thunderbolt. Thus it is no easy labour to war with the sons of Tyndarus. Mighty are they themselves, and of a mighty father were they begotten.

Farewell, children of Leda; and may you ever bless our hymns with fair renown; for dear are all minstrels to the sons of Tyndarus, and to Helen, and to those other heroes who sacked Troy in aid of Menelaos. Your fame, O princes, was wrought by the minstrel of Chios, when he hymned the city of Priam and the ships of the Achaians and the Ilian battles and Achilles, that tower of war. And to you now do I also bring all the charms that the melodious Muses can bestow, and all that my own house has in store. For the Gods, the fairest of gifts is song.

IDYLL XXIV

THE INFANT HERAKLES

Pindar in his first Nemean Ode had recounted in his grand heroic manner the adventure of the infant Herakles with the serpents, and the prophecy of Teiresias concerning his future achievements and deification. Theocritus here treats the same theme in his own more homely but no less vivid style. The poem ends with an account of the young hero's education and training.

O N C E on a time, when Herakles was ten months old, Alkmena
The Midean took him, and the one night younger Iphikles,
And having washed them both and let them suck their fill of milk,
Laid them to rest within the brazen shield, that shapely piece
Whereof Amphitryon had spoiled his slain foe Pterelaos.
Then upon each child's head she laid a hand, and thus she spoke:
'Sleep you, my little babes, a sweet and lightly slumbering sleep.
Sleep, souls of mine, brother by brother, sleep and fear no harm.
Blest be your slumbers now, and blest your wakening to the dawn!'
So saying she rocked the mighty shield, till sleep laid hold of them.
  But when the Bear sinks to his midnight setting, over against
Orion, who now shows a mighty shoulder in the sky,
Then two terrible monsters did the crafty Hera send,
Two serpents, glistening with the speed of their blue-gleaming coils,
To the broad threshold, gliding through between pillar and door,
Urged by the Goddess to devour the infant Herakles.
So creeping out these serpents came writhing along the floor
Their ravenous bellies, and ever as they went a baleful fire
Shone from their eyes, the while they spat their deadly venom forth.
But when they now with flickering tongues had crept near to the babes,
Then did those dear sons of Alkmena waken by the will
Of Zeus the all-knowing, and a light throughout the palace shone.
Straightway when he beheld those evil monsters lift their heads
Over the rim of the hollow shield, and saw their pitiless teeth,
Iphikles screamed, and kicked away the woollen coverlet,
Striving to flee: but Herakles withstood them, and with his hands
Seized them, and in a grievous bondage held them both fast bound,
Gripping them by the throat, just where the evil venom lurks
In baneful snakes, that venom which even the Gods abhor.
Then did those serpents wreathe their coils around the tender child,

That babe unweaned, the nursling who had never shed a tear.
But soon again they loosed their knots, slackening their tortured spines,
As they strove vainly to escape the bondage of that grasp.
  Now through her sleep Alkmena heard the cry, and wakened first.
'Arise, Amphitryon! for terror numbs me and holds me bound.
Arise, stay not to fasten your sandals on your feet.
Did you not hear our younger child, how loud he screamed for fear?
Do you not mark how, though 'tis midnight still, the chamber walls
Are all lit up with a bright light, as though the dawn shone clear?
There is some strange thing in the house, indeed there is, dear lord.'
So spake his wife; and at her words he leapt down from the bed,
And quickly snatched his richly damasked sword, that on its peg
Hung ever ready to his hand over his cedarn couch;
And even as he was reaching forth for his new-woven baldric,
With the other hand seizing his mighty sheath of lotus wood,
Lo now once more with darkness was the wide chamber filled.
Then to his thralls, who still lay snoring heavily, he cried,
'Bring torches hither quickly, lighting them at the hearth,
My thralls: up now, and thrust back the stiff bolts of the doors.'
'Rise, ye stout-hearted serving-men! Rise! Your master calls,'
Cried the Phoenician bond-slave, who slept beside the quern.
The servants now came running in, each with a lighted torch,
And with their bustling to and fro the house was all agog.
But when they saw how Herakles, that little suckling babe,
Was clutching tight those two great serpents in his tender hands,
They shrieked for panic. But the child was lifting the reptiles up
To show his sire Amphitryon, dancing in childish glee.
Then laughing did he fling them down before his father's feet,
Those terrible monsters, sunk by now into the sleep of death.
Alkmena then snatched up and clasped Iphikles to her bosom,
With limbs all stiff for·terror, and his face deadly pale.
But Amphitryon laid the other child beneath a lambswool rug,
Then went back to his bed and there betook himself to rest.
  Soon as the cocks with their third song had welcomed earliest dawn,
Alkmena called before her Teiresias, the seer
Whose word was ever truth, and having told him the strange tale
Of that portent, bade him declare what thence should come to pass,
Saying: 'Even though the Gods desire some mischief, yet, I pray,
Hide it not from me in pity: for not so may men escape

The thread of doom that Fate upon her busy spindle twirls.
But, son of Euēres, let me not teach wisdom to the wise.'
So spake the Queen, and with these words Teiresias answered her:
'Courage, daughter of Perseus, thou noblest among mothers!
Courage, and treasure in thy heart Fate's happier auguries.
For by the sweet light that so long has left my eyes, I swear
That many Achaian women, as they rub the soft wool yarn
'Twixt hand and knee at eventide, shall praise Alkmena's name
In song, and reverenced shalt thou be among the dames of Argos;
So mighty a man this son of thine shall be, who to the mansions
Of the star-bearing sky shall mount, a hero broad of breast,
Whom as their master every beast and all mankind shall own.
After twelve toils achieved, his fate shall be to dwell with Zeus;
But all his mortal part a pyre in Trachis shall devour.
He shall be called the son-in-law of those same deathless Gods
Who sent these serpents from their holes to destroy him when a babe.
Verily soon the day shall come when the fanged wolf, beholding
The couching fawn, shall seek no more to seize him for a prey.[1]
Now, lady, beneath the embers see thou have fire prepared,
And bid make ready faggots of sere thorns, or of brier,
Of brambles, or of pear-tree twigs dried by the buffeting wind;
And on that fuel of wild wood thou shalt burn these two snakes
At midnight, at that very hour they would have slain thy child.
But at dawn let a handmaid gather the ashes of the fire,
Carry them all beyond your borders across the stream, and there
Fling them into some rocky cleft, then let her turn back home,
Nor look behind. Next purify the house with cleansing fumes
Of sulphur first; thereafter take a wool-wreathed branch and sprinkle
Untainted water, mingled, as the custom bids, with salt.
Last unto Zeus, the highest lord, sacrifice a young boar,
That so over your enemies ye may be lords for ever.'
So spake Teiresias, then thrust back his ivory chair, and rose
And went his way, despite the weight of all his many years.

But Herakles, whom men called son to Amphitryon the Argive,
Was reared under his mother's care like a young tree in a vineyard.
It was the ancient Linos who taught the boy his letters,

---

[1] These two lines have been unnecessarily suspected as a Christian interpolation.
Teiresias foretells the coming of a golden age as the result of the labours of Herakles.
We may compare Virgil's fourth Eclogue.

That ever watchful guardian, Apollo's hero son.
Also to draw the bow and send the arrow to the mark
Eurytos was his teacher, rich in broad ancestral lands.
Eumolpos, son of Philammon, was he who made the lad
A minstrel, and to the boxwood lyre disciplined either hand.
And all the tricks of foot wherewith Argive cross-buttockers
Throw one another in wrestling bouts, and all the arts of boxers
Skilled with the gloves, and every wile that rough-and-tumble fighters
To make their science perfect have invented, all these things
Was he taught by Harpalykos of Phanote, the son
Of Hermes, whom no man beholding even from afar
Could find the courage boldly to stand up to in the lists;
So grimly scowled the brow that hung over his savage face.
But to drive forth his horses yoked to a chariot, and guide
The nave of his wheel safely around the turning-post,
That in his loving-kindness did Amphitryon teach his son
Himself: for many a prize had he borne off from the swift races
In Argos, pasture-land of steeds; and he kept unbroken still
The cars whereon he rode, till time decayed their leathern thongs.
And how with spear at rest, and shield guarding his back, to lunge
Against a foeman, or to bide the onslaught of sharp swords,
Or how to marshal a phalanx, or measure with his eye
An enemy's charging squadron, or command a troop of horse,
The knightly Kastor taught him, who had come from Argolis,
Exiled from his whole heritage of broad vine-bearing plains,
When Tydeus from Adrastos received that land of steeds.
No equal in the craft of war among the demigods
Had Kastor, till old age had worn his youthful strength away.
   So thus did his dear mother put Herakles to school.
Meanwhile the lad slept on a bed made by his father's side.
His coverlet was a lion-skin, which gave him great delight.
His dinner was roast meat, and a great loaf of Dorian bread,
A basketful, more than enough for a garden-digger's meal:
But a scanty snack of uncooked food was all he had for supper;
And his plain kilt fell no lower than the middle of his shin.

IDYLL XXV

HERAKLES THE LION-SLAYER

This is a narrative poem in the epic manner, recounting a visit of Herakles to the great cattle-farms of Augeias, king of the Epeians of Elis. It is divided into three sections without connecting transitions. In the first section an old ploughman describes the herds of Augeias to Herakles, and brings him to the farm-buildings: in the second, Herakles, in the presence of Augeias and his son Phyleus, wrestles with and masters a fierce charging bull: in the third part he relates to Phyleus how he killed the famous Nemean lion. There is no mention in this poem of the cleansing of the stables of Augeias, which was one of the twelve labours of Herakles.

The poem is considered by some scholars not to be the work of Theocritus; but there seems to be no sufficient reason for doubting its genuineness.

I

THEN the old ploughman who had charge of the oxen paused from the work that lay between his hands, and said to Herakles: 'Gladly, stranger, will I tell you all that you ask of me, because I dread the awful wrath of Hermes of the roadways, for they say that of all the heavenly Gods his anger is the most terrible, if any man should deny guidance to a wayfarer.

'The fleecy flocks of king Augeias feed not all upon one pasture, nor in one place; but some of them graze by the banks of Elissus, and some along the sacred stream of divine Alpheos, others near the rich vineyards of Bouprasion, and others again here: and for each flock a separate sheepfold has been built. But for his many herds of cattle, overflowing though they be, the pastures hereabouts are ever abundantly sprouting, around the great marsh of Menius; for the dewy meadows and leas are plenteously clothed with the honey-sweet herbage which feeds the strength of horned kine. And this is their one great steading which you see on your right hand beyond the running river, there where the plane-trees grow in a thick grove, and the green wild-olive, a sacred enclosure, my friend, of Apollo of the pastures, the most gracious of deities. And hard by are the spacious shielings built for us country folk, who faithfully keep guard over the great and marvellous wealth of the king, casting the seed into the fallows, that we plough up thrice, or it may be four times in the year. As for the boundary-lands, the toiling vine-planters know them well, and thence they throng to the wine-treading, when the summer has reached its height. For the whole of this plain belongs to wise Augeias, both the wheat-bearing plough-lands and the gardens with their trees, as far as the skirts of the mountain-ridge with its many springs; and over these lands we go to and fro labouring all day long, as behoves thralls, who pass their life upon the fields. But now tell me (and it shall be for your own gain), in search of whom have you come hither? Are you seeking Augeias, or one of those that are his servants? I have the knowledge, and will tell you truly; for indeed I should say that you came of no evil stock, nor yet is there anything of evil seeming about yourself, so mighty a man are you in form and semblance. Verily of such sort are the children of the Immortals when they mingle with mortal men.'

Then thus did the stalwart son of Zeus answer him: 'Yea, old man, it is Augeias, ruler of the Epeians, whom I would fain see: for indeed it was need of him that brought me hither. If now he be at the town among his citizens, busied with his people's affairs, and they are settling suits of law, pray then lead me, reverend sir, to one of the servants, some responsible overseer of these estates, to whom I may tell my quest and hear his answer; for God has made all men to be in need one of another.'

Then did that worthy old ploughman answer him again: 'Stranger, it must be by the guidance of one of the Immortals that you have come hither, so speedily has all that you require been fulfilled. For Augeias, the dear son of Helios,[1] is here, and with him his child, the noble warrior Phyleus. Yesterday he came to the city after many days, to review all the wealth that is his beyond reckoning upon the fields; since even kings think in their hearts that their estate will be the more prosperous if they see to it themselves. But come, let us go to him, and I will lead you to our steading, where we are like to find the king.' So speaking he led the way; but as he looked upon the skin of the beast, and the club that the stranger grasped in his hand, the old man kept pondering as to whence he came; and evermore he longed to question him, but he took back the words as they rose to his lips, in fear lest he should say something out of season, for the man seemed in such haste; and it is hard to read another's mind.

Now as they were approaching, the dogs suddenly became aware of them from afar, both by their scent, and by the sound of their footsteps, and furiously barking they rushed from this side and that upon Herakles, the son of Amphitryon, turning the while to fawn about the old man with aimless yelpings. But he, by just lifting stones from the ground, frightened them and sent them flying to the right-about; then in a rough voice he threatened them all, and checked their barking; yet was he glad at heart to see how well they guarded the steading while he was away. So he spoke thus: 'Yes indeed, what a companion have the mighty Gods created in this beast to dwell among

---

[1] Helios, the Sun-god, was the father of Augeias.

men! and what a heedful creature he is! If he had also intelligence and good sense within him, and could know against whom he ought to show anger, there is no beast could vie with him in merit: but the trouble is just that he is too savage and fond of snarling.' Thus he spoke, and quickly they came to the steading.

II

And now the sun had turned his horses to the West, bringing the hour of twilight, and the fat sheep came flocking in from the pastures to their pens and folds. After them came the kine in thousands upon thousands, like unto watery clouds that are driven along across the sky by the might of the South wind, or of the Thracian North; and there is no numbering them as they journey through the air, nor any end to them, so many are those that the force of the wind rolls up behind those that go before; and rank upon rank they rear their crests in turn: in such multitudes did the kine press forward, herd behind herd. And the whole plain and all the roads were crowded with the moving cattle, and the rich fields overflowed with the sound of their lowing; and the byres were soon filled with shambling cows, while the sheep were being folded within the yards.

Then, of all those innumerable men, there was none who stood idling beside the cattle for lack of work; but one with shapely thongs would be fastening hobbles about their feet, so that he might come close to milk them, while another beneath their dear mothers would be putting the young calves, full of yearning to drink of the sweet milk; one held a milking pail, another was pressing a rich cheese, and another was leading the bulls apart from the heifers. Meanwhile Augeias was visiting every byre, observing the care which his herdsmen bestowed upon his possessions; and along with the king, as he passed through that great wealth of his, went his son, and mighty Herakles, deep in thought. And now, though he bore within him a stalwart spirit, ever firm and unperturbed, yet was the son of Amphitryon astonished beyond measure, when he beheld the uncountable wealth which the God had bestowed. For none would have believed or thought it possible that the substance of one man could be so vast, no, nor of ten besides, even were they the richest of all kings in flocks and herds. But Helios had given to his son this pre-eminent gift, to possess abundance of flocks beyond all other men, and himself ever unceasingly blessed all the cattle of Augeias; for never were his herds afflicted by any of those diseases that destroy the labours of herdsmen; but always more in number, and always goodlier from year to year were the horned kine; for they all brought forth their young alive, and most of their calves were heifers.

Also there went with the cows three hundred bulls, white-legged, with black bodies, and two hundred other bulls of a reddish hue: and these were all of an age for mounting. Again twelve other bulls, besides these, formed a herd sacred to Helios. They gleamed white as swans, and shone out among all the other shambling cattle. These, disdainful of the main herd, grazed by themselves the luxurious grass of the pastures, so marvellously proud were they of heart. And whenever swift beasts came forth from the shaggy oak-forest into the plain, to prey upon the wilder cattle, these were the first, at the smell of the beasts, to go to meet them in fight, bellowing dreadfully, with brows that glanced slaughter.

Now pre-eminent among these bulls in might and strength and proud recklessness, was mighty Phaëthon, whom all the herdsmen likened to a star, because he shone so bright when he went among the other cattle, and was conspicuous afar off. So when this bull saw the dried skin of a tawny lion, he charged straight at watchful Herakles, and would have butted him in the ribs with head and sturdy forehead. But as he came near, the prince gripped him by the left horn with his strong hand, and forced his neck, brawny though it was, down to the ground, thrusting the bull backwards with the whole weight of his shoulder, while on his upper arm the muscle, stretched over the sinews, rose and stood out; so that the king himself marvelled and his son, the warlike Phyleus, and the herdsmen who tended the horned kine, when they beheld the irresistible strength of the son of Amphitryon.

III

And now Phyleus and mighty Herakles, leaving the rich fields behind them, set forth on their way to the town. And after they had hastened to the end of the narrow path leading through the vineyard from the farmhouses, a scarce distinguishable track of green that ran through the trees, and were now come onto the public highway, there the dear son of Augeias thus addressed the child of most high Zeus, slightly turning his head over his right shoulder: 'Stranger, a long while ago I heard a tale concerning you, so at least I guess, now that I call it to mind. For there came hither from Argos a certain Achaian in the prime of his youth, a man from Helike by the sea, who in the hearing of many of our Epeians told this tale, how in his presence a certain Argive slew a wild beast, a terrible lion, that was a dread curse to the country folk, and had his hollow lair beside the grove of Nemean Zeus. "I know not for sure," so the man said, "whether the slayer came from sacred Argos, or dwelt in the city of Tiryns, or in Mycenae." But, if rightly I remember, he said that the man's lineage was from Perseus. Methinks there is none of the Aigialeis[1] who would dare such a deed, unless it be you; and the hide of the beast, which you wear, manifestly proclaims some such mighty achievement of your hands. But now, hero, first tell me, that I may know if my surmise be true or false, whether you are that man of whom the Achaian from Helike spoke in our hearing, and whether I recognise you aright. And tell me how you slew unaided this baneful beast, and how it came to the well-watered region of Nemea; for however diligently you sought, you would not find so great a monster in the whole land of Apia,[2] since it does not breed such huge creatures, but only bears and boars and the fell race of wolves. Therefore all who then listened to the tale, were astonished; and indeed there were some who said that the traveller was lying, that he might gratify his hearers with an idle tongue.'

So Phyleus spoke, and drew away from the middle of the road, that both might have room to walk side by side, and that he might listen the more easily to Herakles, who now came abreast of him and spoke thus:

'O son of Augeias, as to what you first asked me, you have yourself easily perceived the truth aright. But concerning this monster, since you are eager to hear, I will tell you everything, how it all happened, save alone whence he came; for of all the Argives, not one can speak certainly of that: only we guess that some one of the immortal Gods, in wrath for sacrifice neglected, sent him to punish the children of Phorôneus. For over all the men of the lowlands the lion swept like a river-flood, ravaging them insatiably, but most of all the people of Bembina, who dwelt near his lair, and so suffered intolerable miseries.

'Now this was the first labour that Eurystheus charged me to perform, bidding me slay that terrible beast. So I took my supple bow and my hollow quiver, filled with arrows, and set forth, grasping in my other hand my stout club, with the bark unpealed, and the pith still within it, wrought from a shady wild-olive, which I myself had found under sacred Helicon, and had torn up the whole tree with all its branching roots. Now when I came to the place where the lion haunted, I then took my bow and slipped the string over the curved tip, and at once notched onto it a deadly arrow. Then I kept turning my eyes on all sides, on the watch for the baneful monster, if so be I might espy him before he saw me. By now it was midday, and nowhere could I discern his tracks nor hear his roaring. Nor throughout the furrowed seedland was there any man to be seen ploughing with a team of oxen, whom I could question; but pale fear held them all within their farms. Yet I halted

---

[1] The Aigialeis were the Argives.
[2] The land of Apia means the Peloponnese.

not in my search through the thickly-wooded hill, until I saw him and speedily put to proof my strength. Now as evening fell, he came pacing towards his caverned lair, gorged with flesh and blood; and his tousled mane and his gleaming eyes and his breast were all bespattered with gore; and he kept licking his chin with his tongue. At once then I hid myself in the shadowy thicket beside the wooded path to await his coming; and as he came near, I shot at his left flank, in vain, for the barbed shaft did not pierce through the flesh, but glanced off and fell on the green grass. Instantly he lifted his tawny head from the ground in amazement, and looked around him on every side with peering eyes, while his jaws gaped and showed his ravening teeth. So I launched against him another arrow from the string, being vexed because the first had flown from my hand to no purpose; and I struck him in the middle of the breast, where is the seat of the lungs. Yet not even so did the cruel arrow pierce through the hide, but fell before his feet, harmless and in vain. Then yet once more, for the third time, I made ready to draw my bow in fierce disgust of soul; but the furious beast, glaring around him, espied me, and lashing his long tail about his thighs, straightway bethought himself of battle. His whole neck was filled full of wrath, and his flame-coloured hair bristled above his scowling brow, and his spine was arched like a bow, as he crouched, gathering together flanks and loins. And as when a chariot-builder, a man skilled in many a craft, bends the saplings of supple fig-tree, having first warmed them at the fire, to make the wheels of an axled car, and as he bends it, the thin-rinded figwood flies from his hands and springs afar at one bound, so did that terrible crouching lion leap at me from far off, eager to taste my flesh. But I with one hand thrust out before me my arrows and the double-folded cloak from my shoulders, while with the other I lifted the seasoned club above my head, and brought it down on his skull, and broke the hard cudgel of wild olive on the shaggy crown of the ravening beast. Then he fell from on high down to the ground before he could reach me, and stood on staggering feet, swaying his head, for darkness came upon both his eyes, and his brain was shaken in his skull by the force of the blow. So I, perceiving that he was bewildered with grievous anguish, before he could recover breath and come to himself again, made haste to seize him by the nape of his stalwart neck, casting to the ground my bow and broidered quiver. Then, locking my strong hands together, I throttled him with my whole force from behind, lest he should rend my flesh with his claws, and mounting him I trod down his hind feet firmly into the soil with my heels, gripping his sides with my thighs, until I had stretched out his forelegs and lifted him up lifeless, and mighty Hades received his spirit.

'So then I took thought how I might strip his shaggy hide from the limbs of the dead beast, a hard task indeed, since, try as I might, there was no cutting it either with steel or with stone or with wood. Thereupon one of the Immortals put the thought into my mind to rip up the skin of the lion with his own talons. With these I quickly flayed it off, and cast it about my limbs, as a defence against the fury of wounding war.

'Such, my friend, was the slaying of the beast of Nemea, which of late had brought so many a woe upon both flocks and men.'

IDYLL XXVII

THE LOVERS' TALK

The authorship and period of this amusing poem are unknown. It is certainly not by Theocritus. I have omitted the last two lines, as they are meaningless, unless we assume that a number of lines have been lost at the beginning of the poem.

MAIDEN. Helen the wise did Paris rape, just such another neatherd.

DAPHNIS. But here's a willing Helen, claims her neatherd with a kiss.

MAIDEN. Boast not, young satyr; for a kiss is an empty thing, they say.

DAPHNIS. Even in empty kisses there is a sweet delight.

MAIDEN. There, I have wiped my mouth clean, and spit your kiss away.

DAPHNIS. What, have you wiped your lips? Give them again for me to kiss.

MAIDEN. Better for thee to kiss thy calves, than a maid unwed like me.

DAPHNIS. Boast not; for swiftly shall thy youth flit by thee like a dream.

MAIDEN. Though I grow old, yet, while it lasts, this life is milk and honey. Grapes turn to raisins, and not wholly will the dried rose perish.

DAPHNIS. Come hither beneath the olives, that I may tell you a tale.

MAIDEN. No, I won't. You beguiled me with a sweet tale once before.

DAPHNIS. Then hither beneath the elm trees, to listen to my pipe.

MAIDEN. Pipe then for your own pleasure. I hate your dismal tunes.

DAPHNIS. Ah, maiden, have a care. Thou too must shun the Paphian's wrath.

MAIDEN. What care I for the Paphian, so but Artemis hear my prayers?

DAPHNIS. Say not so, lest she smite thee, and thou fall snared in her net.

MAIDEN. If she will, let her smite. Artemis will protect me still. Take back that hand: don't touch me; or else I'll scratch your lip.

DAPHNIS. Thou canst not escape Love, whom never maiden yet escaped.

MAIDEN. Yes, but I do, by Pan. But thou dost ever bear his yoke.

DAPHNIS. This do I fear, lest Love should give thee to some meaner man.

MAIDEN. Many have been my wooers, but not one could charm my heart.

DAPHNIS. Well, I too, one more of those many, hither have come to woo thee.

MAIDEN. And what, my good friend, should I do? Marriage is all vexation.

DAPHNIS. But marriage is not grief and pain; no, 'tis all mirth and dancing.

MAIDEN. Ah, but I'm told that women oft dread their bedfellows.

DAPHNIS. Rather they always rule them. Why, what should women dread?

MAIDEN. Travail I dread. Cruel is the shaft of Eileithyia.

DAPHNIS. But is not thy queen Artemis, who lightens the pains of labour?

MAIDEN. But I dread childbirth for this too, lest I should lose my beauty.

DAPHNIS. If you bear children, you shall see new light dawn in dear sons.

MAIDEN. And what gift worthy of marriage do you bring me, if I consent?

DAPHNIS. My whole herd, all my woodlands and pastures thou shalt have.

MAIDEN. Swear that you will not wed me, then desert me against my will.

DAPHNIS. By Pan, I would not, even should you choose to chase me from you.

MAIDEN. A mansion will you build me, with fine chambers and court-yards?

DAPHNIS. Yes, a mansion will I build thee: and fair are the flocks I pasture.

MAIDEN. But to my agèd father what tale, ah what shall I tell?

DAPHNIS. He will approve thy wedlock, when once he hears my name.

MAIDEN. Come, then, tell me that name of thine. In a name there's often joy.

DAPHNIS. I am Daphnis; Lycidas is my father; Nomaia is my mother.

MAIDEN. You come of well-born parents: yet I am as good as thou.

DAPHNIS. I know it: thou art of high degree: Menalkas is thy father.

MAIDEN. Show me, I pray, thy grove of trees, wherein thy shieling stands.

DAPHNIS. Look yonder; see how tall they grow, my slender cypress trees.

MAIDEN. Browse on, my goats. I must now view this neatherd's land and chattels.

DAPHNIS. My bulls, feed softly, while I show my woodlands to this maiden.

MAIDEN. What are you doing, naughty satyr? Why do you touch my breasts?

DAPHNIS. I'll show thee that these early apples here are growing ripe.

MAIDEN. I shall swoon, yes, by Pan! Take back your hand, please take it out.

DAPHNIS. Courage, dear girl. Why fear me? You are too timorous.

MAIDEN. Don't push me into the watercourse and soil my pretty clothes.

DAPHNIS. Nay, look, my soft sheepskin will I spread beneath your dress.

MAIDEN. Alack, you've torn my girdle too. What did you loosen it for?

DAPHNIS. To the Paphian will I offer it, the firstling of my bliss.

MAIDEN. Stop, wretch. Surely there's someone coming. What's that noise I hear?

DAPHNIS. Only the cypress trees whispering together of thy bridal.

MAIDEN. You've torn my mantle to a rag. I've nothing left to cover me.

DAPHNIS. I'll give thee another mantle, one ampler far than this.

MAIDEN. Yes, all things now you promise: soon not a grain of salt you'll give me.

DAPHNIS. Ah, would that I might fling my very soul down at thy feet!

MAIDEN. Artemis, be not wroth with thy now faithless votaress.

DAPHNIS. I'll slay a calf for Eros, and a cow for Aphrodite.

MAIDEN. A maiden came I hither, and a woman I go home.

DAPHNIS. A woman, aye, and a mother of children, a maid now no more.

So these two lay delighting in the fresh youth of their limbs,
Whispering softly together on that couch of stolen love;
Till at length she arose and sauntered back to herd her sheep.
Her eyes were shamefast, but her heart was filled with bliss; while he
Went back to his herds of kine, rejoicing in his new-won bride.

IDYLL XXVIII

THE DISTAFF

Theocritus, before setting out on a voyage to Miletus, wrote this poem to grace the gift of an ivory distaff, which he was bringing with him for Theugenis, the wife of his friend Nikias, the poet and physician, to whom he had addressed Idylls XI and XIII. The poem is written in the Aeolic dialect, and in the Asklepiad metre. In my translation of Idyll XXX I have attempted as best I can to reproduce this difficult rhythm in English; but in the case of this poem I have found the task impossible without sacrificing more than I should have a right to do of the delicate ease and charm of the original; so I have translated it into an easier but more commonplace metre.

O DISTAFF, thou the spinner's friend, grey-eyed Athene's gift to dames
 Whose careful thoughts are busied with household industry,
Come boldly now along with me to Neleus' bright and glorious town,
 Where green among the delicate reeds the Cyprian's temple stands.
For thither sailing I pray Zeus to grant me favouring winds, that there
I may rejoice my eyes and find a loving welcome with my friend,
 Nikias, that sacred scion to the sweet-voiced Graces dear;
And thee, thou child of toilfully carven ivory, will I bestow
 Upon the wife of Nikias, my gift into her hands,
With whom many a piece of cloth to make men's garments thou mayst work,
 And many a robe of watery fabric, such as women wear.
For twice each year in the meadows would the mothers of the lambs get shorn
 Of their soft wool, might dainty-ankled Theugenis have her way,
So industrious is she, such her zeal for all that prudent housewives love.
 Since ne'er would I bestow thee upon a sloven's house,
Nor on an idle mistress, thee, who comest from my fatherland;
 For thine the town which Archias out of Ephyra founded once,[1]
Marrow of our Trinakrian isle, a city of illustrious men.
 Now shalt thou lodge in a man's house who has knowledge of all drugs
And skilful remedies that keep deadly diseases far from men;
 And in beloved Miletus mid the Ionians shalt thou dwell,
That Theugenis may boast that hers is the best distaff in the town,
 And thou mayst always mind her of her song-loving friend.
For this he'll say that looks upon thee: 'Verily great grace may go
 With a little gift; and precious are all things that come from friends.'

[1] Syracuse was founded by colonists from Corinth, of which the old name was Ephyra. The Trinakrian isle is Sicily.

IDYLL XXIX

The following two lyrics are written in the Aeolic dialect, and have been thought by scholars to be modelled upon lost poems of Alcaeus. However that may be, they are too beautiful to be mere academic imitations, and seem to express, with very genuine sincerity, the passionate friendship of Theocritus for a young man. I have tried, with whatever success, to translate the Greek quantitive metres into English accentual verse.

WINE, dear lad, and the Truth—'tis a saying you oft have heard.[1]
So now we are mellow with wine, we needs must speak the truth.
I at least will tell you what lies in my inmost soul.
You have no wish to love me, not with your whole heart.
I know it; for half my life do I live in the quickening light
Of your beauty, but all the rest is utterly lost and gone.
When you would have it so, like a god do I pass the day
In bliss; but when you refuse me, indeed it is darkness then.
How can you think this right, to torture your lover so?
Nay, if you will but hearken to one who is older than you,
The happier will you be, and will some day give me thanks.
Build for yourself but a single nest in a single tree,
Such that thither no dangerous creeping beast may climb.
For now you perch one day upon one branch, and next day
Flit to another, always in search of something new.
Let but a stranger see you and flatter your comely face,
To him straightway you are more than a three years' friend, while he
Who loved you first, is naught but a comrade of scarce three days.
Is it not too like pride, this spirit you seem to breathe?
Be faithful rather to one true friend your whole life long;
Great praise thus will you win in the mouths of your fellow-men;
Nor yet shall Love ever deal unkindly with you, Love
Whose power can so easily vanquish the minds of men,
And has made me soft and tender who once was hard as steel.
Nay I beseech you by that delicate mouth of yours,
Do not forget this truth, we were younger a year ago,
And no charm may we find that shall save us from growing old
And wrinkled; nor are we able to capture Youth again,
Once it has flown, for the shoulders of Youth are fledged with wings,

[1] The words 'Wine, dear lad, and the Truth' are a quotation from Alcaeus.

And we are too slow to catch a creature of flight so swift.
Then mindful of these truths, all the kinder should you be,
Rewarding with faithful love my faithful love for you.
And so, when you have gotten a manly beard, we two
May be such comrades as once were Achilles and his friend.
But if you should cast my words to the winds to waft afar,
And say in your heart, 'Oh why do you trouble me thus, good man?'
Albeit now I would journey to fetch back for your sake
The golden apples, or Cerberus, watchdog of dead men,
Yet then, though you stood at the doors and called me, I would not stir
One step, for I then should have rest from the cruel pains of love.

IDYLL XXX

A y me, bitter and hard the misery, fierce the anguish of my disease!
Like some tertian ague, love of a boy has racked me a month and more.
Others comelier well may be; but his whole body above his feet
Is naught else but delight and charm, and a sweet smile is about his cheeks.
Though my fever is still fitful, and comes one day and goes the next,
Yet soon there'll be no peace nor respite at all, no not enough for sleep.
Yesterday as he passed he gave me a sidelong glance from beneath his brows:
Shame forbade him to meet my eyes, and his face flushed with a crimson glow.
Love laid hold of my heart then with a grasp firmer than e'er before.
Home I went, with a wound cruel and deep gnawing my heart, and there
Summoned straight to the judgment seat and thus sternly arraigned my soul:
'What is this you are doing, tell me? To what lengths will your folly go?
Know you not that already whitening hairs are showing around your brow?
'Tis full time to reflect that now you are scarce youthful to look on more:
Yet always would you act as those unto whom the savour of life is new.
This moreover forget not: wiser it were henceforth to have naught to do
With such burdensome and disquieting love-desires for a comely boy.
Onward still doth his life speed with the swift pace of a bounding deer;
And next day will he lift anchor and set sail for another port.
Nor yet long mid his boyish mates shall the sweet flower of his lovely youth
Flourish. Ah, but the poor lover—desire still shall devour his heart,
Oft remembering, oft beholding his lost image in dreams by night;
Nor can lapse of a whole year to his stubborn malady bring relief.'
    Such reproaches, and more besides, did I speak sternly against my soul.
But this answer it made: 'Whoso expects to vanquish the crafty, sly

Love-god, truly as vain his folly as if he thought it an easy task
To count how many nines of stars in the skies over our heads there be.
So now, whether I will or will not, I have no choice, but with neck outstretched
Must needs labour to draw the yoke; for the God's pleasure is such, my friend,
Even that God's, who has oft subtly beguiled the sovereign mind of Zeus,
Aye, of the Cyprian goddess too; but a mere leaf of a day, like me,
Needing naught but a breath to lift it, he wafts whither he lists afar.'

THE EPIGRAMS

It is impossible to be certain how many of these epigrams were written by Theocritus. Seven are ascribed in the Anthology to Leonidas of Tarentum as well as to Theocritus (VII, IX, XI, XV, XVI, XX, XXI). Others, such as XII, XIX, XXII and XXIII, are certainly not by Theocritus. The rest may well be his, and they seem quite worthy of being so. I have translated several into prose, because a verse translation of a Greek epigram, if it be not completely felicitous, had better not be made at all. As it is, I fear that I may not escape such censure myself.

The Greek word 'epigramma' means an 'inscription'; but the greater number of the thousands of Greek epigrams that have come down to us were never actually inscribed upon tombs and altars, or beneath pictures and statues: in fact the epigrammatic form became gradually divorced from its original purpose, until it grew to be merely a convenient excuse for writing a short poem. Brevity was essential, but not a witty climax. The modern narrower conception of an epigram is Latin rather than Hellenic.

EPIGRAM I

YONDER dew-besprinkled roses,
And those tufts of bushy thyme
Are dedicated
To the Heliconian maidens;

And to thee, O Pythian Healer,
Are those dark-leaved laurels offered,
Since to honour
Thee the rock of Delphi bare them:

And that white-skinned hornèd goat
Who crops the branch-tips of yon terebinth,
He it is
Who with his blood shall stain this altar.

EPIGRAM II

DAPHNIS white of skin,
He that fluted pastoral ditties
On his lovely pipe, to Pan
Has made these offerings:

His pierced reeds, his crook,
A sharp javelin, a fawn-skin,
And the scrip wherein of old
He carried apples.[1]

---

[1] The apples would be presents for his love (cp. II, 120, III, 10, and XI, 10).

EPIGRAM III

RESTING weary limbs
On the leaf-strewn floor you slumber,
Daphnis, while upon the hill
Your nets are newly staked.

But Pan's following you,
And Priapus, with a garland
Of gold-flowering ivy wreathed
Around his lovely head,

Entering the cave's mouth
Both together. Nay but wake
And flee, oh flee them, shaking off
The drowsy trance of sleep.

EPIGRAM IV

GOATHERD, when thou hast turned aside down yonder pathway through the
    oaks,
    There will you find a newly-carven image of figwood,
Legless and earless, with the bark still on it, yet full well equipped
    Lustily to perform the Cyprian's procreative deeds.
Round it there spreads a sacred garden-close, where gushing from the rocks
    A never-failing streamlet flows, bushed upon every side
With laurels and with myrtles and with sweetly-scented cypress trees;
    And all around the tendrils of the grape-begetting vine
Clamber and creep; while blackbirds in springtide rapture carol forth
    Their varied trills and cadences in clear-voiced madrigals,
And the brown nightingales in answer chant forth their melodious lays,
    And modulate with tuneful bills their honey-throated song.
There sit thee down, and to that kind Priapus pray that I may win
    Deliverance from the pain of loving Daphnis: tell him too,
I'll offer him a lovely kid forthwith. But should he say me nay,
    Three victims will I sacrifice, so I but win his love:
For I will slay a calf, a shaggy he-goat, and a stall-fed lamb
    Which I am rearing. Graciously may the God heed thy prayer.

EPIGRAM V

Wɪʟᴛ thou for the Muses' sake play to me some sweet melody
  Upon the double flute, while I, lifting my lyre, begin
To pluck the strings? Meanwhile the neatherd Daphnis shall enchant our ears
  Awakening with wax-bound breath the music of his pipe.
And so, beside yon shaggy oak, standing within the cavern's mouth,
  Let us rob of his slumbers the goat-pursuing Pan.

EPIGRAM VI

Aʜ miserable Thyrsis, how may it avail thee, though thou grieve
  Till the two sockets of thine eyes are washed away with tears?
Gone is the kid, thy lovely pet; she's dead and down to Hades gone;
  For a savage wolf has snatched her, and crushed her in his claws;
And hark, the dogs are howling. Nay, but what will that avail thee now,
  Since neither bone nor ash is left of her that's lost and gone?

EPIGRAM VII

Aɴ infant son you left behind, and in the flower of your age
  Dying yourself, Eurymedon, beneath this tomb you lie.
With divine heroes now is your abode; but him your countrymen
  Will hold in honour, mindful of his father's excellence.

EPIGRAM VIII[1]

Hɪᴛʜᴇʀ unto Miletus has the son of the great Healer come,
  To succour the physician of diseases, Nikias,
Who ever day by day draws near to worship him with sacrifice,
  And out of fragrant cedar-wood has had this image carved,
Promising with a noble fee to reward for his skill of hand
  Eëtion, who has here put forth his whole art on the work.

[1] This epigram was intended to be inscribed beneath a statue of Aesculapius set up
in his house by Nikias, the friend to whom Theocritus addressed Idylls xi and xiii.

EPIGRAM IX

STRANGER, this the advice
Syracusan Orthōn gives thee:
Never go forth after drinking
On a stormy night:

For such fate was mine.
Therefore, far from my own native
Land, here am I lying buried
Deep in alien soil.

EPIGRAM X

YE Goddesses, for the delight of all you nine has Xenokles
    Set up this marble altar: a true musician he,
(As no man will gainsay), who since he has won glory by his art,
    Does not forget the Muses, to whom his thanks are due.

EPIGRAM XI

BENEATH this stone lies Eusthenes, the physiognomist and sage,
    He who had skill to read the very spirit in the eyes.
Nobly his comrades buried him, an alien in an alien land,
    And his dear friend was the poet who wrote this epitaph.
All funeral dues and obsequies to the dead sage have now been paid;
    And poor weak mortal though he was, he had friends to weep for him.

EPIGRAM XII[1]

IT was the choir-master Demomeles
Who dedicated this tripod to thee,
Dionysus, dearest of the blessed Gods.
In all things was he temperate; and he won
Victory with his choir of men, because
He had regard for beauty and seemliness.

---

[1] This epigram was inscribed on a fourth-century Athenian tripod. It is not likely that Theocritus wrote it, but it is attributed to him in the Anthology.

EPIGRAM XIII

THIS is the Cyprian—not the Vagrant Goddess. Worship her
By her name 'Heavenly.' It was chaste Chrysogone who set up
Her statue in the house of Amphikles,
Whose children and whose life she shared; and ever
Yearly more happiness was theirs, since they began each year
With worship of thee, Goddess. For mortals who are mindful
Of the immortal Gods, are the more fortunate themselves.

EPIGRAM XIV

With citizens and foreigners this counter deals impartially.
    When the accounts are balanced, draw your deposit out.
Let others make excuses; but Kaïkos pays back money lent,
    Aye, even after nightfall, if so you should desire.

EPIGRAM XV

I shall know, wayfarer,
Whether you honour most the good, or hold
The base in like esteem.

'Hail to this tomb,' you'll say,
'Because it lies so light above the head
Of blest Eurymedon.'

EPIGRAM XVI

UNTIMELY in her seventh year this maiden passed to Hades,
When all her youthful prime was still to come.
Poor girl, for her small brother she was pining: not yet twenty months
He lived before he tasted loveless death.
Alas, woeful Peristera! How very near to men
Has Heaven set the miseries we most dread!

EPIGRAM XVII[1]

UPON this statue gaze with heed, O passer-by;
   Then, when home to your country you return, say:
'Anacreon's image once at Teos I beheld,
   Greatest singer of all the ancient poets.'
And if you add that in the young was his delight,
   You'll have truthfully thus described the whole man.

EPIGRAM XVIII

DORIAN is the speech, and Dorian the man I praise, Epicharmos, the inventor of comedy. To thee, O Bacchus, the Koans who are settled in the city of Syracuse, have set up in bronze the image of the living man, because he was their fellow-countryman. Doubtless mindful of his wise sayings they paid him this recompense; for many things profitable unto life did he say to their children. Great thanks be his.

EPIGRAM XIX

THE servant of the Muses, Hippōnax,[2] lies here.
If thou shouldst be a rascal, draw not near this tomb.
But if thou art a true man, of good parents born,
Boldly sit down, and, if thou wilt, drop off to sleep.

EPIGRAM XX

IN memory of his Thracian nurse
Little Medeios built this wayside tomb,
And thereon he inscribed her name, Kleita.

This one sweet recompense is hers
For all her careful nurture of the child.
And what's that? Still a good servant is she called.

---

[1] I have here tried to reproduce the metre of the original. The second line of each couplet is a hendecasyllable.

[2] Hipponax was a satirist who wrote in the sixth century B.C.

EPIGRAM XXI

STAY and behold Archilochus, the ancient poet, the maker of iambics, whose infinite renown has spread to the regions of the sunset and of the dawn. Surely the Muses and Delian Apollo loved him well, so melodious was he, and so skilled both at writing verses and singing them to the lyre.

EPIGRAM XXII

YOU see here Peisander[1] of Kamīros, the man who first of the ancient poets wrote of the son of Zeus, the lion-slayer, the swift of hand, and told the tale of all the labours he accomplished. Know that it is he whose likeness the people cast in bronze and set up here, when many months and years had gone by.

EPIGRAM XXIII

THE inscription will tell what tomb this is, and who lies beneath it: 'I am the grave of the famous Glauke.'

---

[1] Peisander was an epic poet of the seventh century, who wrote a poem about Herakles, which is now lost.

Printed in the United States
By Bookmasters